Published by Familius LLC, www.familius.com

Familius books are available at special discounts for bulk purchases for sales promotions or for family or corporate use. Special editions, including personalized covers, excerpts of existing books, or books with corporate logos, can be created in large quantities for special needs. For more information, contact Premium Sales at 559-876-2170 or email specialmarkets@familius.com.

Library of Congress Catalog-in-Publication Data   2015935373   pISBN 978-1-939629-69-2

Edited by Lindsay Sandberg   Cover and book design by David Miles

Photo credits: 6, 8, 10, 13, bottom details on 103, and 170–173 by Christy McCullough; 14, 24–31, 133, 174–188, 190, cover elements, photo backgrounds, and decorative elements from Shutterstock.com; all other photographs by Mike and Debbie Schramer and Adam and David Miles.

10 9 8 7 6 5

First Edition

How to Make Amazing Fairy Furniture,
Miniatures, and More from Natural Materials

MIKE & DEBBIE SCHRAMER

fairy house

FAMILIUS

Dedicated to mothers, fathers, and
children of all ages who love the woods
and the fairy tales they inspire.

Acknowledgments

We would like to express our deep gratitude to Christopher Robbins for his belief in the beauty of this book, to Lindsay Sandberg for her many tireless hours of editing, and to David Miles, whose artistry in book design helped make our creative vision a reality. We are grateful for everyone at Familius whose kindness and faith in our book helped make our first book a wonderful experience.

We want to thank our sons, Michael and Matthew, who were the adorable little people in our lives when we created our first little chair from nature. They have always been the brightest joy in our lives. Their wonderful talents and creative abilities constantly amaze and inspire us. We are grateful that they are following their own creative dreams: Michael in his unique and amazing music compositions, and Matthew in his creative and inventive film endeavors. Their confidence and energy as artistic people help us to believe more in ourselves.

We were also blessed by the kindness of Debbie's parents, Normand and Barbara Poulshock, and we are thankful for the many inspiring years spent on their little farm, where our artistic journey began. Their life and love of music also brought many years of joy to our lives. We especially want to acknowledge Barbara, whose love of beauty and artistry truly inspired us as she constantly encouraged us to use our own creative energies.

Mike's mother and father, Bonnie and Joe Schramer, and his many brothers and sisters were always a source of warmth and love. Many of his mother's encouraging words about his art were a comfort to him that he still remembers and holds dear to his heart.

We would also like to acknowledge Rebecca Hoffberger, founder and director of The American Visionary Art Museum, for her sensitivity to our work and for valuing our story, our unique talents, and our spirits. Rebecca gave us the incredible opportunity to share our art with hundreds of thousands of people through her museum's wonderful exhibits. She is a gentle soul, and her understanding and appreciation of art go far beyond that of anyone we have ever met.

Lastly, we want to thank our many wonderful friends, fellow artists and those who have collected our art over the years. We are truly grateful for the encouragement they have given us throughout our art career.

Contents

Preface

We began creating our nature art in the late 1980s, and since that time, many people have expressed their hopes that we would write an instructional book to highlight our art and also demonstrate how it is created. Our art and our story have developed a great deal since then. But it wasn't until our son Matthew introduced our art to Christopher at Familius that our long-awaited dream of writing this book came true.

In *Fairy House*, we share our experiences as husband-and-wife nature artists with over twenty-five years of making beautiful miniature art forms that actually resemble real-life objects. We relate anecdotes and stories from the perspective of our lives as working artists and from our relationship with nature. One of the most pleasant experiences of writing this book was revisiting our fond memories of living on a small farm in the Northwest where our artistic journey began.

One important motivation for writing this book was to help people find their creative inner child. We hope to touch the hearts of people, young and old, and to help them find happiness by using more creativity in their lives. As our lives intertwined with nature for over twenty-five years, we were made the beneficiaries of many awakenings about life, beauty, and the humble spirit of the earth. We still look forward with excitement to what new dreams and visions we will have to create an even more beautiful and childlike world through our art and our story. It is our sincerest hope that you will feel and experience these same joys of creating with nature. It is also our purpose to inspire you to create new and memorable experiences with nature that will continue to bless and comfort you throughout your life.

In this unusual book, we will glean from our years of experience as nature artists; we will share with you how to gather, preserve, and use found and recycled natural materials collected from gardens, forests, fields, and the sea. We will demonstrate how to turn these beautiful treasures into amazing little furnishings, enchanted cottages, and tiny accessories from the fairytale realm. *Fairy House* will help you to discover the artistically gifted person you truly are, to see beyond creative boundaries and expectations, and to use the innate artistic abilities you have within you so abundantly.

As an artist working with nature, you will begin to see a different world than you had ever noticed before. Working up close with flowers and bark, stones and shells, and all the other many materials in nature, you will be given a deeper appreciation of these beautiful natural objects. If you let the beauty of nature inspire you and speak to you in its gentle way, your talents will emerge to give you a comforting peace and joy. Nature has a language that can teach us and guide us, as people and as artists.

There need not be as much perfection in creating art from nature as is often required in doing other forms of art. Indeed, the look of imperfection and even a quirky, offbeat naturalness might express more of the real feeling of this kind of art than trying to make something precise or perfectly in line. That is why we encourage you to go about this adventure with unrestrained creativity and to have fun. Because this is a more expressive art form, imagination is more important than perfection.

Debbie and Mike exhibiting The Fairy Castle in Brooklyn, New York.

What You'll Learn

What you will learn specifically in this book is presented in a very detailed, thorough, and imaginative way. You will be able to learn what materials to look for in nature for your art and how to gather and preserve them. You will learn the basic construction techniques that you will need to create your pieces and how you can embellish and decorate them. In *Fairy House*, we also share wonderful suggestions about working with natural materials and the easiest, most productive way to utilize them. We will help you to develop your own artistic ideas for your pieces, too, by sharing ways to accomplish specific steps and how we have made some of our pieces that may be similar to your ideas.

We will also teach you how to see the potential in nature for artistic creativity by looking at a pod and learning how to fashion it into a tiny teapot or by seeing the unique texture and line of an unusual piece of driftwood and learning how it can be turned into an awning for your forest cottage. We will share with you how to make chairs, tables, bookshelves, beds, cradles, and many other amazing and intricate pieces. Also, you will learn how to make the smallest creations: tiny accessories for your pieces, such as little dishes, teacups, books, paintings, sculptures, and all the little comforts of home. As these emerge from your new artist's hands, a delightful transformation will undoubtedly take place in your little world of fairyland.

In one of the most exciting projects, after learning the basic skills of nature art, you will learn how to make a wonderful little Forest Cottage to house all of your little natural furniture pieces. You will also learn to make several little Woodland Characters from nature.

Fairy House is a beautiful book, filled with lovely gems of wisdom about the imagination and creative spirit in each of us. It is an instructive and joyful adventure of learning and artistic discovery that will amaze and surprise you. You will learn how to look at nature and use your imagination to fashion an artistic miniscule kingdom, fit for a king and queen. We also hope our book inspires you to spend more time out in nature and to feel a renewed and lasting love for this beautiful world. As a greater and perhaps unexpected reward, you will experience the joys of working up close with nature's beautiful and intricate details and design in a more unusual way.

Gathering and Preserving Natural Materials

I n this first section, we will share our ideas and suggestions on how to gather, grow, and preserve materials from nature to create a useful palette for your art. You will also learn how to identify the natural materials you will use and how to find them, searching the forest, fields, gardens, and the sea. We will also discuss what general materials and tools you will need to gather before you start creating your own fairy art.

The Necessities: Your Fairy Art Tool Kit

Working with nature to create beautiful art requires just a few basic tools for each project, and several others on occasion. Here are the basic tools you will need to use for all your nature art:

A	Hammer	**E**	Utility knife		Ruler
B	Saw	**F**	Tweezers		Carpenter's glue
C	Chisel	**G**	Scissors		Two-part epoxy
D	Glue sticks and hot glue gun	**H**	Pruners		Paintbrush and basic paints

Discovering and Gathering Nature's Treasures

Nature has such an amazing and vast array of flowers, trees, plants, shells, stones, herbs, grasses, and other beautiful objects; it is truly an inspiring world, whether you are just an observer or someone who wants to create from it. Both skills, observing and creating, work together in a harmonious and helpful way. By being open to the intricacy of nature and seeing every detail, an artistic person can glean many creative ideas from looking at nature up close. In this section, we will share the adventure of gathering. Here, you will be able to learn what flowers, pods, twigs, branches, leaves, and moss to look for. (The next section will help you learn *where* to find these materials.)

All of the natural materials listed here can be gathered in the wild or grown in gardens and preserved; they can also be purchased from suppliers (which we have shared in Appendixes A and B).

FLOWERS

A	Ranunculus	**F**	Rose	**K**	Globe amaranth	**P**	Purple coneflower
B	Aster	**G**	Strawflower	**L**	Baby rosebud	**Q**	Chamomile
C	Sunflower	**H**	Zinnia	**M**	Carnation	**R**	Amaranth
D	Hydrangea	**I**	Statice	**N**	Bougainvillea	**S**	Larkspur
E	Poppy	**J**	Bells of Ireland	**O**	Delphinium		

MOSS

A Dark green sponge moss	**C** Chartreuse moss	**E** Sponge moss	
B Lichen	**D** Icelandic moss		

BARK

A Magnolia	**C** Paperbark maple	**E** Cherry	**G** Fir
B Strawberry	**D** Hawthorne	**F** Holly	**H** Birch

SEEDS, PODS, AND OTHER DRIED MATERIALS

A   Cattail down
B   Skeletonized Japanese lantern
C   Dried avocado skin
D   Cinnamon stick
E   Japanese lantern
F   Tomatillo skin
G   Milkweed pod
H   Sycamore seed pods
I   Tomatillo leaf skeleton
J   Juniper berries
K   Dried mushroom pod
L   Nigella peed pod
M   Thistle seed pod
N   Dried lime
O   Craspedia flower
P   Dried cantaloupe seeds
    (strung on fishing line)
Q   Eucalyptus gum nut pod

R   Eggplant caplet
S   Protea seed pod
T   Poppy pod
U   Sequoia cone
V   Carob pod
W   Pine tree seed pods
X   Chestnut tree seed pod
Y   Flame tree pod
Z   Sweet gum tree seed pod
AA Cotton pod or caplet
AB Waratah seed pod
AC Eucalyptus pod
AD Bottle tree seed pod
AE Gum tree pod
AF Lotus seed pod
AG Grapevine tendril
AH Kurrajong tree pod
AI Gum nut seed pod

AJ Wallichi seed pod
AK Beech tree pod
AL Baby lotus pod
AM Acorn
AN Eucalyptus pod cap
AO Eucalyptus bell pod
AP Hakea pods
AQ Macrocarpa flower seed pod
AR Iris seed pod
AS Hazelnut pod
AT Banksia pod
AU Bushy Yate pod
AV Eucalyptus bud
AW Australian leaf pod
AX Stick bottlebrush pod
AY Flowering gum pod
AZ Australian pod
BA Sheoak pod

ROCKS AND SHELLS

A Fluted clam shell

B Sea glass

C Rock

D Mussel shell

E Polished rock

F Coral

G Limpet shells

H Broken shell

I Turret snail shell

J Worm shells

K Part of a starfish

L Cockle shells

M Deep shell

N Japanese Babylon shell

O Candy stripe snail shell

P Rice shell

Q Cat's Eye shells

R Gulf Oyster drill

PAPER AND SEEDS

A Brown tracing paper

B Printed sheet music

C Corrugated cardboard

D Rosehips, berries, and seeds

E Sewing pattern

F Handmade paper

LEAVES, BRANCHES, AND VINES

A   Maple leaf

B   Australian dried leaf

C   Leaf skeleton

D   Ginkgo leaf

E   Protea leaf

F   Eucalyptus leaf

G   Gum tree leaf

H   Lunaria leaf

I   Australian cupped leaf

J   Oak leaf

K   Pink eucalyptus leaf

L   Fern leaf

M   Lamb's ear

N   Cottonwood leaf

O   Grapevine branch with tendril

P   Fruit tree branch

Q   Driftwood

R   Fir tree branch

S   Banana stalk

T   Winged elm branch

U   Cholla tree branch

V   Cottonwood branch

W   Seaweed

X   Manzanita branch

FABRIC AND ODDS AND ENDS (OPPOSITE PAGE)

A   Antique metal
B   Jewelry flower
C   Polished rock
D   Colorful rock
E   Coiled metal
F   Buttons
G   Mirror pieces
H   Metal piece from beach
I   Crystal bead
J   Old leather

K   Crystal
L   Photograph negatives
M   China shard
N   Stained glass
O   Glass buttons
P   Metal chains
Q   Delicate wire
R   Antique trim
S   Antique floral ribbon
T   Taffeta

U   Beaded silk
V   Antique silk
W   Sequined cord
X   Glass bead netting
Y   Floral fabric
Z   Antique braided ribbon
AA   Gold Ric Rac
AB   Sheer wired ribbon
AC   Velvet ribbon
AD   Fabric with metal jangles

SEAWEED AND KELP

A   Thin seaweed strand
B   Kelp stem
C   Seaweed strands

D   Coiled seaweed
E   Kelp bulbs
F   Sea onion

G   Kelp with thick outer layer

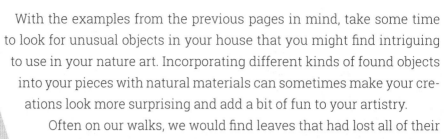

With the examples from the previous pages in mind, take some time to look for unusual objects in your house that you might find intriguing to use in your nature art. Incorporating different kinds of found objects into your pieces with natural materials can sometimes make your creations look more surprising and add a bit of fun to your artistry.

Often on our walks, we would find leaves that had lost all of their greenery; we call them "leaf skeletons." These are the delicate, lacy framework of leaves. They can be found in the layers of leaves on the ground below trees, usually best gathered in the spring. We have used these in many inventive ways. A great aunt of Mike's who lived in Illinois shared her childhood memory of how she and the other children in the neighborhood would pour syrup on the green leaves they had gathered. They would then set the leaves out so the ants would eat all of the syrup and the flesh of the leaves, leaving a leaf skeleton still intact.

Gathering Techniques

FORAGING TIPS: WHEN AND WHERE TO GATHER

1   After a storm is good time to go for a walk to discover what has been brought down by the wind or what the sea has left behind through the storm's turbulent waves.

2   Try to gather materials that have finished their blooming cycle and have fallen to the ground. If you cannot do this, gather plants that are still growing, but try to do so with restraint to allow enough of the plants to remain and thrive. Always gather from nature with kindness, for this gentle world that we live in is as alive and growing as we are.

3   Gather during any season or time of the year. Flowers, in particular, are best collected in the late morning, after any dewdrops have dried. Flowers usually bloom in early or late morning, or sometimes midday, depending on the type of flower; wait until the peak time of the day to pick them. Remove any excess moisture on the petals or the flowers will mold and become disfigured.

4   When you are gathering the flowers without the stems, use a container that has good ventilation, such as a loosely woven basket (preferably with a handle for easier collecting), so the air can get through the reeds of the basket to aerate the flowers. Using a basket works well for gathering flowers that are somewhat flat, such as pansies and California poppies. It is best to have only one layer of flowers in your basket in order to prevent crumpling.

5   As you gather flowers or other plants, cut the stems long enough so that they can be tied into small bunches, at least six to ten inches (the length of the stem should be proportionate with the

weight of the flower so that it holds up well in your art). If you are going to collect a large quantity of plants, you can bring a long branch, then tie the bundles to it, carrying it horizontally so the flowers or herbs will hang upside down from the branch. They will start drying right away and will be ready to hang up when you return home.

6   Be aware of plants that might be poisonous or perhaps might cause an allergic reaction. Study the list of poisonous plants in your area or where you might be collecting, and learn how to identify them so you can avoid gathering these by mistake.

7   Vacant fields can also yield a good harvest of wild flowers, herbs, and other plants. Be sure to leave most of what is there, taking just enough that you can work with, so that the field can replenish itself and keep growing beautifully.

8   Your own gardens can be the most rewarding place of all to gather materials for your nature art. Gathering from what you grow yourself will make your pieces even more special.

WHO TO ASK

1   There are many people who would be excellent resources for obtaining natural materials. You may have friends or neighbors that have gardens who might be willing to share some of their cuttings with you or let you collect from their yards. Even community gardens may be happy to help you. The most important thing, however, is to always ask permission from the landowner, if you can, before gathering natural materials.

2   It is illegal to collect anything natural from parks or other public places. However, you can talk to a park ranger or other employee to see if they will give you permission to gather a few things to use in your art. We have occasionally asked rangers at state parks if we could collect small bags of driftwood for our artistic purposes and have often been granted permission. The rangers always appreciate being approached about gathering from their park rather than finding that someone has taken plants or twigs without asking.

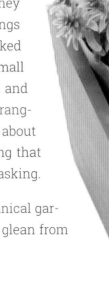

3   Gardeners at colleges, universities, and botanical gardens typically accommodate our request to glean from their property's clippings.

4   Landscapers and tree pruning companies are often willing to share branches, plants, and other natural materials that they have cut as well. We have even be given materials from contractors who were bulldozing land to make way for new buildings.

Preserving Nature's Beauty

Preserving the beauty of nature is an amazing process; you will now be able to see how all your hours of careful gathering will give you beautiful and useful treasures with which to create! Here we will explain three ways of drying your flowers, leaves, and herbs, but if you want to experiment with other methods, there are many books and websites which are helpful in learning these processes as well. Also, experimenting on your own, using the different materials you find, can have good results; sometimes the best methods of preserving natural materials comes through trial and error. Just remember to keep a simple record of your discoveries about preserving the materials you've gathered so that you can replicate the process.

AIR DRYING:

This is the most frequently used method of drying and preserving flowers and plants. The purpose of drying flowers is to give the moisture in them time to evaporate; that is what preserves them so they will last indefinitely. Also, quite simple and foolproof, air drying is fun and will most always yield wonderful results. You will need to use flowers that are still on their stems for this technique, so gather up the flowers that you have collected in this way and set them on a table.

1   If you had already made small bunches of flowers or herbs while you were collecting, then part of your work is done. If you did not bundle your flowers while on your nature walk, you can do this now. Just take a small grouping of flowers and bunch them together, wrapping a rubber band or string around the stems—fairly tightly—as the stems shrink slightly as they dry.

2   Tie a piece of string up horizontally in a dark, dry room—free of humidity—to hang the flowers from, or, if you have rafters in your attic, you can hang bunches of flowers from nails in the rafters. Keep the groups of flowers spaced apart as much as possible to leave enough room for the air to circulate between them.

3   As an alternative, you can hook a paper clip into the rubber band that is holding your flowers together, then attach the paper clip onto the string or the nails. You will need to hang them from the stems so that the flowers are upside down; this way, they dry more completely and keep their shape better.

4   Depending on the types of flowers that you are drying and the temperature in the room, leave your flowers, herbs, or other plants to dry for five to six days.

5   To determine if your flowers are dry, feel the texture of the petals. If they feel papery and sound crinkly, then they are ready to take down from their drying area to use.

6   If you don't use them immediately, leave the dried flowers in a dark, low-humidity room. They can also be placed in boxes for storage and kept on a shelf in a room that is dry as well.

Most flowers, leaves, and herbs with long stems respond very well to this type of preservation. Roses especially dry beautifully in this way. White flowers dry a little paler than when they are fresh but are still pretty. Normally, herbs do not take quite as long to dry as flowers, but it depends on the type of herb and how thick and porous the leaves are. Trial and error is often helpful here. Drying the herbs upside down in a dark, dry, humidity-free room yields the best results. Bachelor's buttons, Bells of Ireland, milkweed, and iris seed heads dry very well with this method.

WATER DRYING

You may have observed fresh flowers in a vase of water becoming dry and crackly after several days. This is a natural way of drying flowers. Purple coneflowers, roses, hydrangeas, tulips, iris, daffodils, chamomile, mint, and borage all dry beautifully in water.

1   Gather your flowers or herbs and set them loosely into a vase full of water.

2   Leave them in the vase for four to six days, replenishing the water if it evaporates or is gone before the flowers are completely dry.

3   When the petals or leaves feel leathery or papery, remove them from the vase and store them in a box or hang them upside down in a dark, dry place until you are ready to use them.

DRYING WITH BORAX

This is probably our favorite way to dry flowers, leaves, herbs, and other plants.

YOU'LL NEED:

One 4-pound box of borax

Two 2-pound boxes of white cornmeal

2 tablespoons salt

Long, rectangular cardboard box or plastic box

Fine, delicate paintbrush or makeup brush

Sturdy storage container (to store the mixture when you aren't using it)

1   First, make sure your flowers, herbs, or leaves are completely dry and free from moisture.

2   Organize the flowers, herbs, or leaves you are going to dry; this will make it easier to identify them when they are covered with the borax mixture.

3   Mark both the names of the materials that you are drying and the date you started drying them on the box you use.

4   Mix the borax, white cornmeal, and salt, then pour an evenly distributed layer into the cardboard or plastic box. If the flowers that you are drying are fairly flat, the layer can be just 1/4 inch thick. Normally, most flowers take between five to six days to dry completely in the borax mixture, similar to the previous drying methods. A dark, dry, and moisture-free room is also needed to use this drying method.

5   Place the flowers in the borax mixture at least 1/4 inch apart from each other in a single layer.

6   Next, cover the flowers with the Borax mixture, being very careful not to disturb or move the flowers as you cover them. Make sure the petals do not fold over as you do this.

7   If you want to dry flowers that are more bell-shaped, thicker, or wider, then you will need to add up to a half inch of mixture into the bottom of the box. To dry flowers that are bell-shaped, such as Canterbury bells or tulips, turn the flower so that the bell shape is facing up and push the flower gently into the drying mixture until it almost reaches the bottom of the box. Then, very gently pour more of the borax mixture into the bell shape of the flower and cover the rest completely.

8   Leave the flowers in the mixture for five or six days in a dry place. Do not disturb the flowers or move them at all while they are drying; they do best if they are left to dry in the borax without any disruption.

9   After six days, carefully remove the flowers by hand or with a thin spatula, picking them up from underneath, not by the petals. Before you use or store the flowers, use your fine paintbrush or makeup brush to very carefully dust off the remaining dry mixture on the petals.

10 Again, store your now preserved flowers or other materials spaced apart from each other so the air will circulate between them and so they will not become moldy or damaged. An enclosed box with a lid works best to keep out moisture.

Almost every variety of flowers, herbs, and leaves preserves well using the borax mixture. Some that we particularly enjoy drying in this way are cosmos, pansies, Cantebury bells, hollyhocks, herb leaves and flowers, and maple leaves.

PRESSED FLOWERS

Pressing is quite an easy way to preserve flowers as well as leaves and herbs. Commercial flower press kits are available at many craft and department stores, and some specialty art supply shops, if you would like to use something more professional. You can also just use large, heavy books to press your flowers and leaves, which works fine, too. It should be a book that is not valuable or of sentimental meaning to you, however, since pressing flowers in books can somewhat affect the binding. Phone books work very well, too, especially because the paper is thin and absorbs the moisture of the flowers well.

1 Prepare your flowers, leaves, or other materials by dusting them gently with a fine paintbrush or makeup brush.

2 Then, simply place the flowers down onto one of the pages of the book, keeping them spaced apart so they do not overlap.

3 Start by pressing your flowers in the center of the book first, then choose pages further away from the center pages for additional flowers. Make sure there are enough pages in between the flowers you are pressing that the weight of the paper will help press the petals.

4 Leave the flowers in the book for three or four days.

5 Then, carefully remove the flowers from the pages. Take care not to tear the petals or dislodge them from the center of the flower itself.

6 Pressed materials can be stored in a moisture-free box, following the same steps as we mentioned in the previous preserving methods. It is also best not to layer the pressed flowers or leaves; instead, create just one level of the material to prevent any damage. Store your pressed items in a dark, dry room with low humidity as well.

One last tip: To keep your dried flowers from fading and to retain their beautiful colors, you can spray them with a floral fixative, which can be purchased at craft stores. Both hair spray and an acrylic, matte finish spray work well. If you do not want to use any kind of chemical spray on your flowers or leaves, keeping them away from sunlight or heat will help.

We remember many things from the wonderful walks we have taken together. The gentle, green hills and meadows were filled with lovely flowers of every color. The forest seemed to speak softly as we walked over lush moss and lichen. When you walk about in the outside world, you will discover this same gentle world. Everywhere you look in nature, you will see amazing and intricate artistry. The earth is filled with life and energy. An artist can see, hear, and feel this world and create from it with great respect and admiration.

As you prepare to start your nature art, remember to enjoy the magic of being in nature and preserving that which is naturally beautiful.

Making the Basic Elements

Throughout our book, we suggest ways of working with nature, but if you discover a technique that feels more comfortable for you, use your artistic judgment. Now, onto the actual process of making your beautiful little fairy furniture! First, we will talk about gluing your pieces together.

Basic Techniques

GLUING

There are two different techniques for gluing.

METHOD 1:

You can apply hot glue to the end of one branch then attach the end of another branch, holding them together for about ten seconds to let the glue set.

METHOD 2:

Alternatively, you can set both branches down on your table, glue the ends together, and then hold them in place until the glue sets.

USING MOSS

Always apply glue to the undersides of chairs, tables, bookshelves, or other pieces you make to give them more strength, and then cover all the glue with moss. Using a hot glue gun works best for making nature art, but without the moss, the glue is not as strong. The moss works as a bonding material, especially when you use it to cover all of the glue.

Rolling the moss into tighter pieces keeps it together when you need to cover very small areas; however, you can let the moss be a little fluffier when adding it in larger amounts. Tweezers are also very helpful when adding moss or other materials to areas that are difficult to reach or when you are working on tiny pieces. When the glue is set and you have your moss in place, look carefully for any "glue threads" or visible glue showing through your materials. (Glue threads are the thin, string-like strands that pull away from the applied glue as you take the glue gun away.)

If you use moss to cover all of the areas where you apply glue and then remove the glue threads, your work will appear more magical and pleasing to the eye. You do not want the viewers to see signs of your work; the moss will make your creation seem more natural.

To use "creative thinking" is as important as actually making something; it is what helps you develop your inner talents and artistic abilities.

MAKING A "SQUARE OF BRANCHES"

1 Cut four branches the same size (about 2 1/2 inches by 2 1/2 inches) and lay them down on your table, gluing the branches together at all four corners. Be careful not to get glue on the table or surface you are working on so that the branches can be lifted up easily.

Let the glue set until it is dry (usually about eight to ten seconds).

2 Put moss over the areas you have glued to make the corners stronger. Press the moss down carefully.

Turn the square over and repeat, gluing and adding moss to the other side. This extra step assures that the piece will be sturdy and stay together better.

3 Cut seven or eight branches the same length and size as those which made the frame. Starting from one side, glue the branches down side by side, filling the empty space until you've covered the entire square. Secure the branches to the frame on both ends with glue and moss.

MAKING A "RECTANGLE OF BRANCHES"

Using the same steps suggested in making the square of branches, you can construct a rectangular frame that can be incorporated into a bench, a loveseat, a couch, and so on. And remember, it doesn't have to be perfectly straight. As long as the basic rectangular shape is there, it can still be somewhat off center, angular, or disproportionate; this adds uniqueness to your work.

Furniture Tips

FURNITURE ARMS

To make arms for your chairs, benches, and loveseats, it is a good idea to choose some interesting materials that will enhance the rest of your piece. Try holding up different kinds of materials to your basic framework to see what might look best before gluing anything on. When you've found the piece of seaweed, twig, or grapevine tendril that looks perfect, glue it on, adding moss over the glue when the piece is secure.

HEADBOARDS

To make a headboard for a bed or cradle, there are so many different ideas you could use. It all depends on how you would like your piece to look. If you want to create a wispy, delicate piece, then use thinner, smaller branches, vines, or tendrils. You could make the headboard simple or it could be very elaborate. We try to let the natural materials we choose spontaneously inspire us to create the design or look of a piece.

Decorating Your Pieces

It is best to wait to decorate your piece until it is finished, but if you think of ways to embellish your creation as you go along, set the materials you have in mind beside you to help you remember. Learn to add beautiful flowers, leaves, herbs, and tiny shells to your lovely pieces; these pretty, natural materials will make your works of art bloom with detail and fascination.

We hope that you will feel truly inspired when creating from nature and that your pieces will reflect the love you have for this beautiful world. Every person has so much talent within them. This kind of art can help bring out the skill and vision that you have within you.

Perhaps the most important part
of creating with nature is to let
its beautiful spirit speak to you, to
hear its story and voice.

A Little Chair

C reating a chair is a wonderful place to start. Think for a moment about all of the things we do as we sit in chairs. Gather up the tools and natural materials you will need, and find a nice area to set out your supplies to begin creating. Then, once you have an idea for the chair you'd like to create, choose the branches, flowers and pods that would compliment your vision.

YOU'LL NEED:

A   Square of branches (covered with moss or bark) for the seat

B   Four branches for the legs

C   Twigs or another material for armrests

D   Piece of bark or rectangle of branches for the chair back

E   Moss

F   Pods, tendrils, and flowers for decorating

1 Create the basic square of branches (see page 34). If the branches you are going to use are very thick, we suggest cutting them with pruners; if they are thin and delicate branches, you can use scissors.

You can also consider using a piece of bark, some leaves, or shells.

2 To add chair legs, turn the seat of the chair over so the bottom is facing up. Hot glue the four branches, one by one, to the four corners of the seat. Cover all the glue with moss.

3 Add braces or rungs to the legs of your chair to make it sturdy. There are several different ways to do this. One way is to glue a branch across from one leg to the other, adding these rungs (like the rungs on a real, life-size chair) to all four legs and then covering the glue with moss.

4 You can also add bracing or rungs to your chair across the gap between two legs at a diagonal. Or you could add additional rungs by crisscrossing branches between the legs.

5   Create the back of your chair using a rectangle of branches, a piece of bark, or leaves.

Glue the bottom of the back of the chair to the back of the seat of the chair. Be sure to use enough glue so that the pieces will hold together well, and then add moss over the areas where you have glued. Hold the pieces together carefully while the glue sets.

6   Add the armrests (using bark, leaves, tendrils, kelp, or twigs).

7   Decorate the finished chair. Decorating your piece makes it more unique and gives it personality to become a real work of art. Embellishing your chair can be an elaborate part of your creation, or you can keep it beautifully minimal.

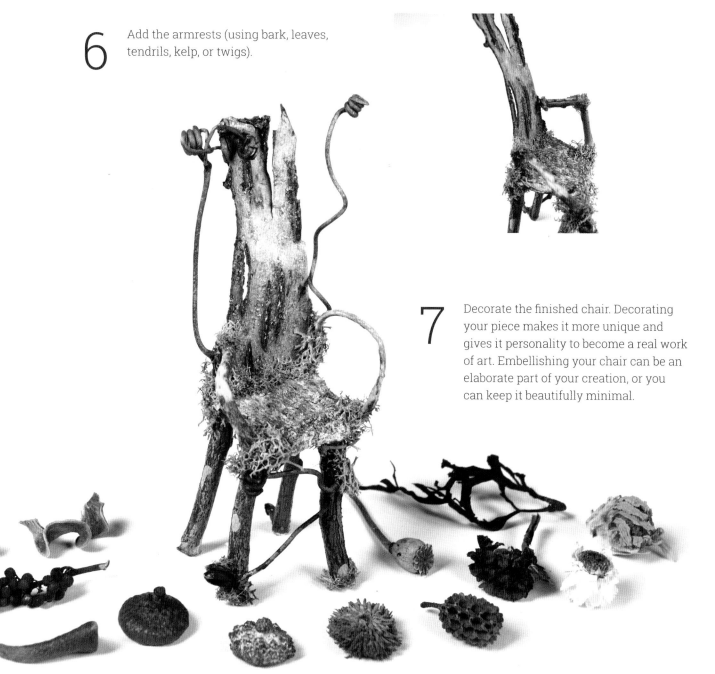

Now you have created a beautiful work of art from nature! We hope this has been a wonderful, exciting, and fun experience for you. You started out using very basic elements and learned to create beyond that first step to make something that you are hopefully very happy with. If making your first piece was somewhat difficult, however, try again, be patient, and see what else you can do. The more you create with nature, the better your skills will become. We can remember when we began our adventure in nature art . . . at first, we struggled a little, trying to keep the branches together, but soon, we forgot how difficult it was because the pieces we were making became so magical and amazing! That will happen for you, too.

DECORATING IDEAS & VARIATIONS

Here are some examples of other kinds of chairs you could make showing the natural and found materials we used to create them.

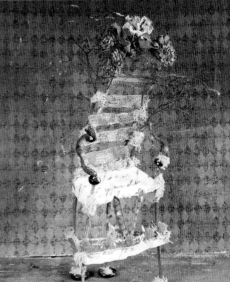

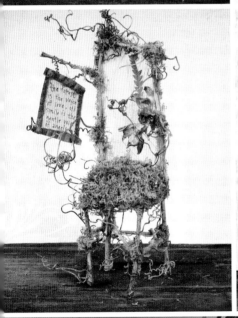

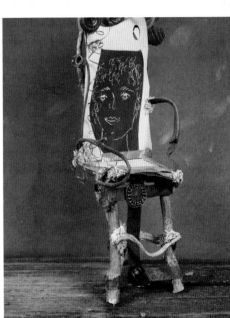

Use nature in a way that best
highlights or honors it and that will
bring attention to it in a beautiful way.

A Fairy Table

with Accessories

ables add so much charm to any set you make. You can create tables that are breakfast tables for two, set with bowls and spoons, or great tables for a fabled feast. You can make quiet tables for reading with candlesticks and books or writing tables with lamps and tiny inkwells with quill pens.

YOU'LL NEED:

A Square or rectangular bark to serve as the tabletop surface

B Four branches of equal length for the table legs

C Four smaller pieces of bark, each equal in length to one side of the tabletop

D Four or more branches to serve as braces

E Moss

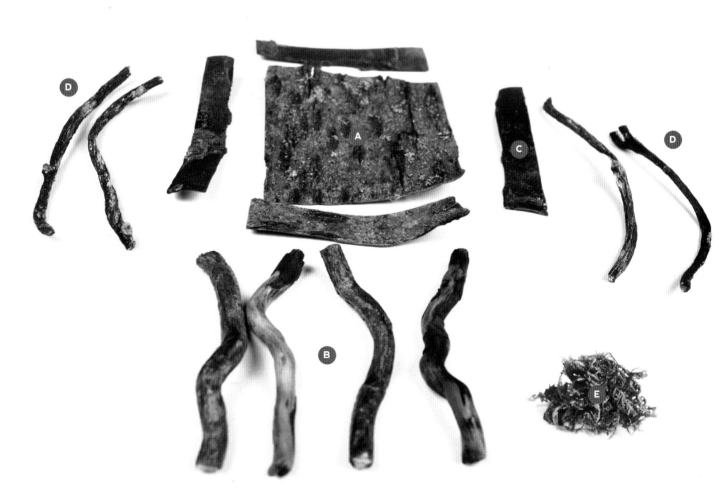

1 Prepare your tabletop, either by cutting bark down to the appropriate size or by making a square or rectangle of branches.

2 Turn the tabletop over to glue the legs to the corners of the table. Hold each leg as you glue it until the glue sets, and then cover each glued area with moss.

3 For a decorative look, add the smaller pieces of bark along the edges of the tabletop. This gives the table a more finished look.

4 Glue straight or curled braces to the legs of your table. Cover all of the glued areas with moss, and remove any glue threads. Inspect your table for sturdiness.

Accessories

Make some tiny accessories for your table. A teapot, a teacup, a vase of flowers, and a bowl of berries or fruit are just the beginning.

A TEAPOT

YOU'LL NEED:

A   Poppy pod or acorn for the body

B   Small, curved grapevine tendril for the handle

C   Curved twig or pod or the end of a sea onion for the spout

D   Pod or berry for the lid

E   Moss

1   Prepare a pod that has the shape of a teapot. Eucalyptus pods, gum tree pods, and acorns work well. Trim off the top of the pod to make a spot for the teapot lid to be added later.

2   Glue both ends of the grapevine tendril to one side of the teapot for the handle, holding it in place until the glue is dry and covering the glue with moss.

3   Glue the pod or curved twig to the opposite side of the teapot to make the spout. Again, hold it in place until the glue sets.

4   Glue the pod or berry to the top of the teapot. Cover all remaining glued areas with moss.

A TEACUP

YOU'LL NEED:

A   Acorn, sea onion, or anything spherical for the cup

B   Small tendril or other curved twig for the handle

C   Open pod, round piece of bark, or thick leaf or flower for the saucer

D   Moss

1   Cut the acorn or sea onion in half very carefully with scissors to make a cup shape. Glue the grapevine tendril to one side of the cup for the handle.

2   Cut a thick leaf or a piece of bark into a small circle for the saucer, or you can make the cup without the saucer. The saucer can be separate or you can glue it to the base of the cup.

3   Cover all glued areas with moss and remove any glue threads.

A VASE

YOU'LL NEED:

A   Sea onion or pod for the vase

B   Thick leaf or piece of bark for the bottom of the vase

C   Small flowers with stems

D   Moss

1   Trim off the top part of the sea onion or pod to make the body of the vase.

2   Glue the leaf or piece of bark to the bottom of the vase. The base does not need to be much wider than the vase.

3   Glue the flowers into the vase.

4   Add moss to all the glued areas before placing the vase on your table.

A BOWL OF BERRIES

YOU'LL NEED:

A   Open acorn or eucalyptus pod

B   Berries: juniper, rose hip, Oregon grape cluster, etc.

1   Place the berries into the bowl. You can use different seeds, tiny shells, stones, or twigs to look like fruit, vegetables, or other foods for your bowl.

Your table can be any size and shape and made of any material so it feels perfect for your fairy guests.

DECORATING IDEAS & VARIATIONS

Chairs and writing desks go
together to create a space for us to
think, to dream, and to share.

The Poet's Writing Desk and Chair with Accessories

There is something very special about working at a desk where you can have your pens and pretty papers close by, perhaps a book to read or write in, and a lovely lamp brightening the room. A special writing desk might have small shelves or compartments above the desk surface to save letters in or to display tiny sculptures or photographs that inspire the writer or reader.

Making a Poet's Writing Desk

YOU'LL NEED:

A Piece of bark, driftwood, or flat shell for the desktop

B Four branches for the legs

C Seaweed, tendrils, or vines for leg braces

D Bark for the back of shelves and faux drawers

E Seaweed or bark for decoration

F Moss

G Pods for decoration

1 Make a rectangular table, following steps 1–4 on page 44. It is best to use material that will give your writing desk a solid surface.

Helpful Hint: You can use cardboard to make a template for the desktop and then use that template to trace the shape onto your natural materials.

Glue the piece of bark along the back edge of the desktop to form a backboard.

2 Along the backboard, glue groups of tiny open shelves or pods together to form the little compartments. Add moss to all glued areas, then decorate desk with pods, vines, and moss.

Making a Chair

Using the materials and steps from A Little Chair on page 38, make the chair for the Poet's Desk.

Next, we will share how to make the accessories for the Poet's Writing Desk: a book, an inkwell, sheet music, and a little lamp. Making these accessories is really fun and will add more detail and enchantment to this piece. Try to make it look as if you had just been sitting there, writing a story or reading a book, but had walked away to get a cup of warm chamomile tea.

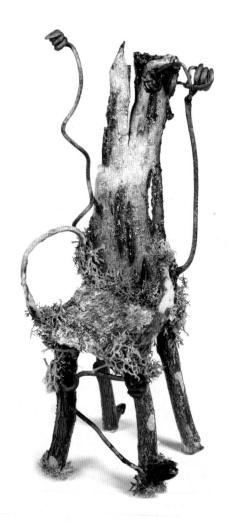

Accessories

BOOK

YOU'LL NEED:

A   Old leather or pliable bark (cherry, birch, or palm)

B   Pages from an old book or sheet music

1   Cut the leather or bark into the shape of an open book, which you will fold to put the pages inside. This will be the cover of the book.

2   Cut little pages that you can fold over; these should be slightly smaller than the book cover. You could also use textured blank paper for the pages of the book to make a tiny journal; add verses, illustrations, or even a map; or glue tiny, reduced pictures onto the pages.

    Helpful Hint: To make the pages of the book more interesting and unique, look for old handwritten sheet music at garage sales, thrift stores, used book stores, or antique shops. The more faded and old the sheet music is (or any kind of paper), the more enchanting and aged the book will look.

3   Glue the pages into the center of the cover.

4   Make a latch for your little book by cutting a thin piece of leather or bark and gluing one side onto the back of the book. Then bring the piece around to the front, glue it down, and cover the glue with a small bit of moss. You can even add a small clasp, a tiny bit of old jewelry, or a beautiful bead to make it more magical. If you want your little book to actually open, you would need to make the latch detachable on one side rather than closing the book completely.

5   Your little book can be picked up and used, or you can glue it onto a table or a bookshelf.

AN INKWELL AND A QUILL PEN

YOU'LL NEED:

A   Small pod, sea onion, or bell-shaped flower

B   Peacock feather

1   Choose the shape you would like to use for your inkwell. It should be smaller than the book you've just made. Cut the top of the shape to leave an opening for the pen if it doesn't have an opening already. If the inkwell isn't flat on the bottom, add a little piece of driftwood or a thick leaf so it sits well on the desk.

2   Use a tiny feather for the quill pen, or cut small pieces from a larger feather. (Peacock feathers work very well). Put glue on the end of the feather and insert it into the inkwell. Add moss to the bottom of the inkwell and glue it to your desk. (You can add an inkwell to other pieces in this book, as well.) Be sure to cover any glue that shows with moss.

SHEET MUSIC

YOU'LL NEED:

A   Handwritten or printed sheet music

1   This is probably the simplest accessory to make—just cut a little grouping of handwritten or printed sheet music into a small square or rectangle shape. Then glue the small pages onto your table or even a little music stand.

A LAMP

YOU'LL NEED:

A   Gum tree pod

B   Bougainvillea flower petals, Japanese lantern pod, dried Canterbury bell, Bells of Ireland flower, sea onion, or leaf skeleton

C   Eucalyptus pod, twig, piece of driftwood, thick tendril, or shell

D   Small, decorative flowers

E   Moss

1   Glue the eucalyptus pod to the top of the gum tree pod to hold up the lampshade.

2   To make the lampshade, glue Bougainvillea flower petals onto the eucalyptus pod in a layered fashion (or attach a Japanese lantern to the top of the twig or glue layers of leaf skeleton onto a poppy pod).

3   Add a small piece of bark or a flat stone onto the bottom of the pod for a base so that your lamp will stand up well.

4   Cover all the glue with moss, then decorate your lampshade with tiny flowers or shells.

DECORATING IDEAS & VARIATIONS

You can adjust the instructions for this piece to make a dressing table or vanity; just make the same kind of desk and add a back with shelves and a little mirror. If you do this, you will then have the opportunity to make little hairbrushes, combs, jewelry boxes, and bottles of lotion or perfume. What else can you think of?

In a canopy bed, you feel like
you are a little princess, sleeping
in a faraway magical land.

The Princess Canopy Bed

C anopy beds conjure up so many dreams. We once created a beautiful canopy bed for a wedding gift. It was soft and covered with an antique wedding veil, ivory beads, and tiny stars. But the most amazing part of this lovely piece was a painting on the bottom of the canopy bed of a couple floating in the air above a meadow of flowers.

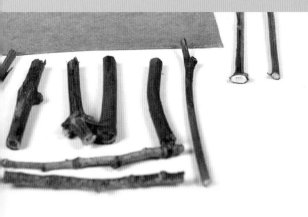

1   Cut a basic rectangle from bark, wood, or cardboard in the size and shape you want your bed to be. You can also make the bed frame completely from twigs rather than using bark or cardboard; this will take a little longer, but it looks more natural.

2   Cut four branches, twigs, driftwood pieces, or pieces of a similar material of equal size for the legs and glue them to underside frame of the bed. It is a good idea to choose branches that are thicker or wider at the bottom so that the bed will stand up well. You can also glue pods as feet on the bottom of the legs, which will make the bed look more grounded and stable.

3   Cut four more branches for the posts of the headboard and the footboard; they don't need to be the same height (the headboard can be taller than the footboard to make it a little more unique). Make all four branches tall enough to accommodate the space between the bed itself and the canopy. Glue the four bedpost branches to the bed frame at each corner.

4   Brace the legs to make them stronger by adding rungs. You can do this in several different styles. Do you want to have a more modern, linear look, or a more curved look? Take time to go through your materials and see what you can find that might make your bed really beautiful and unique.

5   Create the bedding or mattress before covering or enclosing the canopy so you have more unrestricted room to work. The bedding or mattress can be fashioned from thick moss, rose petals, or pussy willows. You probably want the bedding to look very soft and fluffy, so add enough moss or whatever material you choose. If you use rose petals or pussy willows for the top of the bedding, you can glue down a layer of pillow stuffing first. Then put a piece of fabric over that and add the rose petals, pussy willows, or even cattail down, which is very soft. You can also make bedding by creating a pillow in a rectangular shape the size of the bed and filling it with lavender, rose petals, or herbs for a lovely, fragrant mattress.

Cover any areas where the glue shows with either moss or flowers.

Glue the little mattress you made onto the bed, unless you have glued your bedding material right onto the bed frame or over stuffing of some kind to make it fluffy.

6   Connect the four bedposts at the top, which will complete the basic form of the canopy. Glue delicate tendrils from one bedpost to another so that there are four branches supporting the canopy. The canopy does not need to be boxy; you can use curly or more curved branches or twigs that are somewhat irregular. The canopy can have a pyramid shape, an oval shape, a very straight design, or something wavy that uses curly willow or curly filbert branches.

7   Add something lacy, like a leaf skeleton or fabric netting. It can be tied in the corners or hang down, depending on how you want your canopy to look.

DECORATING IDEAS & VARIATIONS

Embellishing the canopy for your Princess Bed can be very
artistic. Every part presents an opportunity to add flowers,
grapevine tendrils, tiny shells, or polished stones. If you've
gathered clematis or Virginia creeper vines, you can wrap them
around the posts and the canopy. Have fun and make it look
amazing!

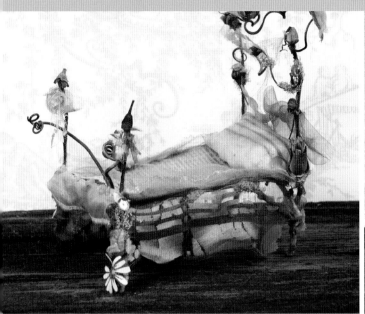

Rocked in a cradle with a
sweet lullaby, a baby fell asleep
in his beautiful dreamland.

The Woodland Rocking Cradle

I t is so special to make a cradle because it represents children and brings about sweet feelings and memories. So as you create your little woodland cradle, remember the children who have touched your heart; perhaps their gentle spirits will be reflected in the beautiful artistry you share.

YOU'LL NEED:

A Bark, a thick leaf, or cardboard for the bottom of the cradle

B Cattail down, pussy willows, moss, or flowers for the bedding and mattress

C Four branches, or sturdy vines or leaves, to brace the sides of the bed

D Moss

E Poppy pods or one square shape for the head-board and another for the footboard

F Four small, sturdy branches for the legs

G Two curved branches to make the cradle rock

H Small branches for braces and supports

I Flowers, pods, leaves, and shells for decoration

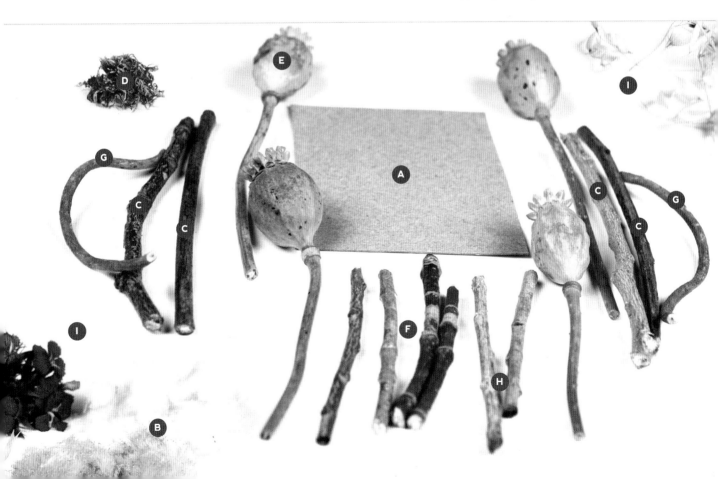

1 Choose a material for the base of the cradle that will look nice on the bottom, since it could show as the cradle rocks. Perhaps you could paint a little picture there as a surprise, as we did on the wedding bed we created.

To make the headboard and footboard, you can use poppy pods or cut unique branches—like curly willow or birch branches—to serve as the posts on each of the four corners of the base of the cradle. Make the branches of the headboard slightly longer than those for the footboard. Remember that the base will have the mattress or bedding on it, so it will be a little higher when it's done.

Glue the poppy pods at each corner of the base of the cradle. Add crisscrossing tendrils or curled vines to give your cradle a more wispy feeling. Wisteria, morning glory, and sweet pea vines are wonderful options for this type of effect.

2 Cut strong branches for the legs. These should be quite sturdy but not so thick that they detract from the delicateness of the rest of the frame. Use enough glue to make sure the legs will stay attached to the cradle, and then cover the glue with moss. Check to see that the cradle is level when you set it down on a table.

3 Add the bracing for the legs. Add moss over the glue.

4 Next, add the sides to the cradle. Attach any kind of sturdy stems, branches, or vines from the headboard to the footboard to glue them together. These will act as bracing, just as in making a chair or table. Be sure to use enough glue so that these areas are strong, and cover the glue with moss.

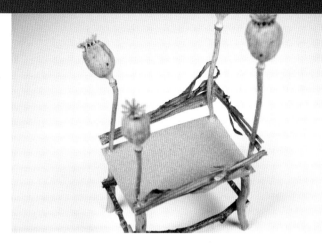

5 To make the headboard and footboard of the cradle look more finished, add wild grasses in between the poppy pod headboard posts. Just cut the length you need, then glue the ends of the stems onto the bed frame, covering the glue with moss when you are done.

6 For the bedding and mattress of the cradle, set beautiful moss or pussy willows into the space for the bedding. You could also use cattail down, cottonwood fluff, or various kinds of flowers for the bedding; anything soft and delicate is perfect for a cradle.

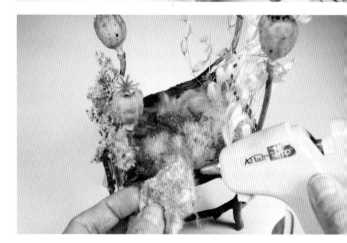

7 To make a pillow, use cattail down or wrap a little circle of moss with fresh lamb's ear leaves. Form the pillow shape first with the moss, then glue the lamb's ear leaves on, using the glue somewhat sparingly. The leaves are delicate, and the glue will show through them if too much is used. Then add a few small flowers or reindeer moss around the edges of the pillow.

8 You could also add a colorful pillow with beautiful Sweet William flowers. Just glue the flowers onto the bedding, and cover the glue with moss.

9 Before you add the rockers, decorate the cradle with flowers, fragrant herbs, tiny shells, or whatever else inspires your imagination. There are many different ways you can decorate your cradle; you can make it very simple or very elaborate. Embellishing your piece makes it come to life.

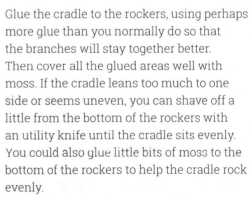

10 The final step for the cradle is to at last add the rockers. First, temporarily set the cradle onto the curved branches to see where you will need to glue the legs to the rockers. The rockers will stay attached to the cradle legs better if the ends of the legs are cut at the same angle as the curve of the rockers.

Glue the cradle to the rockers, using perhaps more glue than you normally do so that the branches will stay together better. Then cover all the glued areas well with moss. If the cradle leans too much to one side or seems uneven, you can shave off a little from the bottom of the rockers with an utility knife until the cradle sits evenly. You could also glue little bits of moss to the bottom of the rockers to help the cradle rock evenly.

At this point, check to make sure everything looks finished and that the cradle rocks nicely and does not fall over when you set it down.

Your lovely little cradle is done! We can only imagine how beautiful and special it is. We hope that by following the instructions we have shared in these first few projects, you have found happiness in creating your wonderful fairytale art. It is a joy for us to know that you are discovering this amazing, miniature world of beauty!

VARIATION IDEA

*The hushed feeling of quiet in a library
brings out our reverent, gentle natures.*

King of the Elves Bookshelf
with Accessories

Bookshelves are found in every castle and hobbit's house. They will artistically display your handiwork. They can hold vases, bowls, stacks of plates, pots and pans, little musical instruments, and of course, books. If you make a library in your fairy house, you could create a bookshelf that is as long as the back wall of the room.

YOU'LL NEED:

A   Three rectangles of branches, or rectangular pieces of bark or leaves, for the shelves

B   Four fairly long branches to serve as the posts

C   Six shorter branches the width of the bookshelf for supports for the shelves

D   Four long branches for the braces

E   Moss

1 Cut four branches the same size to use for the posts of the shelf and set them aside. They can be whatever height and width you would like.

Make three rectangles of branches, or measure and cut three rectangular shapes out of bark, a thick leaf, or any other kind of flat material for the actual shelves.

2 Glue three small branches of the same length to the longer branches to connect the post branches for the shelves. The smaller branches should each be the same width as the actual shelves. Using two of the posts, make a three-rung ladder shape with the connecting branches at the levels where you want the shelves to rest. Repeat this step to make a second ladder shape. Use enough glue so that each area will be sturdy. Then cover and strengthen with moss. This is the basic frame for the bookshelf.

3 Glue the bark or branch shelf pieces onto the ladder framework at each rung.

4 Add bracing for the bookshelf. Attach branches in the areas that will help support the shelves the best. Cover all the glue with moss and remove any glue threads that remain.

Your bookshelf frame is finished, so now you can have the fun of decorating it. You can attach leaf skeletons to the back of the bookshelf, which will show through the branches and create a very pretty look. Gluing grapevine tendrils here and there on your bookshelf will give it a more interesting and whimsical look as well. Adding pods, lichen, or tiny stones would make it a more rustic and earthy piece.

Accessories

Now you can make the accessories for your little bookshelf. Here are just a few interesting objects that you might want to create. You can also create books, sculptures, or other little musical instruments.

A VIOLIN OR MANDOLIN

YOU'LL NEED:

A   Sturdy paper or thin cardboard for templates

B   Cherry or birch bark for the instrument body

C   Small pieces of bark for spacers

D   Bark or a thick leaf for the sides

E   Pod or flat stone, shells, or tiny piece of driftwood for the bridge

F   Morning glory or strawberry vines, threads, or wire for the strings

G   Moss or lichen

1   To make a violin, draw the shape (including the neck) onto a piece of sturdy paper or thin cardboard; cereal box cardboard works well. Cut this shape out, then trace the shape onto cherry or birch bark. Do this step twice to make a top and a bottom piece for the instrument.

2   Cut and glue small pieces of bark here and there on the bottom violin piece; these should be as wide as you would want the violin to be. These act like spacers between the top and bottom pieces of the violin.

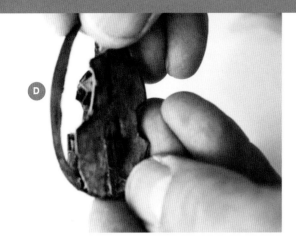

3 Glue the top and bottom pieces together by putting glue on the ends of the small spacers you just added. Be sure to use enough glue so that the two sides stay together well.

Cut thin strips of cherry bark and glue them around the sides of the violin to hold it all together.

Cover all the glue with moss or lichen.

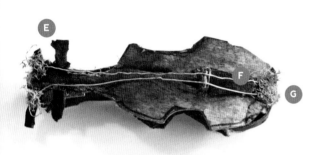

4 Cut a little bridge out of bark. Make notches in it for the strings, then glue it down on the front of the violin to hold up the strings.

Attach small branches, tendrils, or pods to form pegs at the top of the violin.

Glue several pieces of thin wire for the violin strings to the pegs and over the bridge, and then attach them to the tailpiece. Cover all the glue with moss.

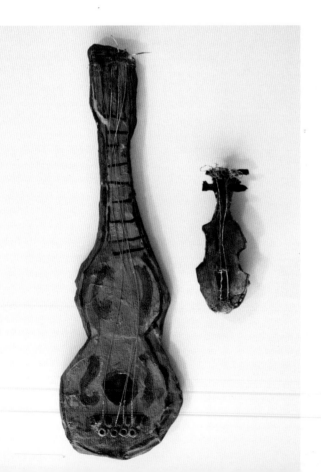

Helpful Hint: You can make any stringed instrument this way. A mandolin would have a rounded back; use a round pod or shell for this part.

FRAMED PICTURES

YOU'LL NEED:

A Small leaf, thin bark, or paper to use for painting

B Tiny, reduced photographs or drawings

C Thin strips of bark to make the frame

D Small branch to make a stand

1 Paint a picture onto the leaf or bark, or glue on a miniature photograph or drawing.

2 Glue the bark strips around the edges of the picture. You can also use tendrils or tiny shells.

3 Add a tiny branch on to the back of your picture so it can stand upright on a table or shelf, or glue your pictures to the walls of any room in your cottage.

AN EASEL

YOU'LL NEED:

A Three long branches for the legs

B Three short twigs for braces

C Twig or piece of bark for a ledge

1 Glue three long, equal-size branches together at the top, creating a tripod shape.

2 Brace the three branches with the small twigs, gluing the ends of each brace to a different branch.

3 Glue a twig or a piece of bark to the front of the easel to make the ledge that will hold the painting or framed picture.

Use a twig to make the paintbrush handle. For the bristles, you can use doll or horsehair. Use bark or a leaf for the painting canvas.

You can be a true forest gatherer by walking gently through every lovely area you find, cherishing each pretty treasure in nature and sharing it with others through your beautiful, unique art!

Dresser for the Forest Gatherer

This dresser brings to mind a little forest elf walking through a beautiful, green forest, foraging for lovely leaves and little twigs, pods, flowers, and berries. A gatherer is someone who is deeply touched by each delicate object they discover in the forest, by the sea, or in a meadow of colorful flowers.

YOU'LL NEED:

A   Branches to make bookshelf shape for frame of dresser

B   Thin balsa wood or bark to cover the frame and for shelves

C   Small branches for braces on dresser frame

D   Longer branches for drawer braces

E   Various pods for teapots, cups, and bowls

F   Moss, tendrils, flowers, herb leaves, seeds, and berries for decoration

White acrylic paint and a paintbrush (not pictured)

1 Construct a bookshelf frame using steps 1–3 from the King of the Elves Bookshelf on page 68. Be sure that you make only the frame, no shelves. Glue the branch braces in a T shape on all four sides of the frame as shown to use as supports for the drawers. These areas need to be level, since the drawers will slide into the top and bottom spaces. Make sure the braces are glued on well, and cover the glue with moss.

2 Make the back of the dresser where the shelves will be attached out of a rectangular piece of balsa wood or bark. Cut the balsa to roughly 4 inches high by 5 inches wide, with a rounded top edge. Two shelves fit nicely onto this space.

3 Cover the branch framework of the dresser with balsa wood or thin bark pieces. Glue the pieces onto the back, the sides, and the top, leaving the front open and using enough glue to make sure the balsa wood or bark stays on well. Trim any extra wood if necessary and add moss over any visible glue.

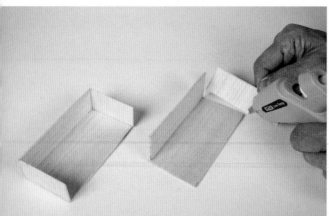

4 For the drawers, make two box shapes that are open in the front and on the top. To get the dimensions right, measure the area where the drawers will go. Cut the appropriate pieces from balsa wood or bark.

Glue all the sides and bottoms together, then cover the seams with moss. Test the size of the drawers by sliding them into the supported area; adjust as necessary.

5   To finish the drawers, cut a front piece of balsa wood or bark for each drawer. Make the front pieces a little bigger than the drawers so they will be even with the frame of the dresser.

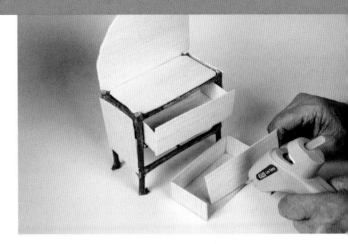

6   If you want to paint the dresser, now is the time to do so. If you have used bark to cover your dresser frame, try leaving a little of the bark showing through the paint to give your dresser a distressed, aged look. Paint the drawers separately, then put them back in the dresser when the paint is dry. The shelves and supports can be painted as well.

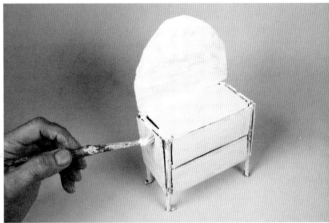

7   Lastly, add the shelves. Cut bark, balsa wood, or cardboard in long rectangular panels, one a little larger than the other to distingush the top and bottom shelves. Before gluing the shelves on, test them to see if they will fit on the back support area. Glue small branches into two ladder shapes onto the dresser and back support as shown. Then glue the shelves to the branches and to the back support, and cover all the glue with moss.

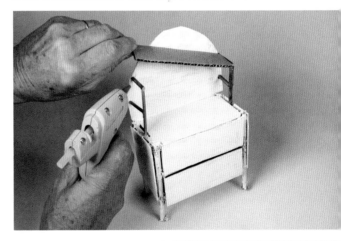

8   Decorate the framework of the dresser with leaves and moss, add handles to the drawers, and add little teacups, teapots, and other dishes. Embellish your piece using your imagination and vision.

This little dresser is one of those pieces that brings out the child in everyone. Think of the tiny treasures you can keep in your dresser, and display them in a beautiful way!

Your creations may be used by the
fairies and elves in Netherland,
which is neither here nor there.

A Couch Made for Angelic Conversations

A couch can be a loveseat, a bench, a tête-à-tête, or a porch swing. Similar to the chairs you have already made, a couch will have the same basic design but will be longer so that two people (or two elves, gnomes, or fairies) can sit on it.

YOU'LL NEED:

A Two long and two short branches to create a rectangle of branches (see page 34)

B Two short branches for the front legs

C Two long branches for the back legs

D Leaves, moss, or petals to create the backrest

E Branch the length of the seat for the back brace

F Two tendrils or curved branches for the armrests

G Twigs or tendrils for braces between the front and back legs

H Flowers, ribbon, beads, and coiled metal for decoration

1   Prepare the material for the seat of the couch or loveseat. Cardboard or bark work well, or you can make a rectangle of branches.

Cut four branches for legs; two should be longer to make up both the legs and the support for the backrest. Try to choose branches, twigs, driftwood, or other materials that look unique or unusual; the front legs, especially, should look different and can add a lot of character to your piece. Glue the legs to the corners of the seat you have just made (underneath the couch). Make sure that the front legs are glued to the underside of the seat and the frame is secured to the back legs with moss and glue.

2   Now glue bracing or rungs onto the couch between each leg to make your piece stronger. You can use unique twigs, tiny pieces of driftwood, thick flower stems, or anything you choose. Glue the bracing on and cover with moss.

Glue the arms to the sides of the couch about halfway up the back, and attach the other end of the tendrils to the seat on the front corners.

3   Cut a branch the length of the couch to serve as a brace for the backrest. Glue the branch on both ends to the top of the back legs and cover the glue with moss. Fill in the back of the couch or loveseat. Attach a row of lovely fern fronds, leaves, or feathers to the back of the couch, and cover the seat with pussy willows, tiny shells, or flowers. The back of the couch could be wispy and delicate compared to the seat or very detailed with a row of little twigs.

4 Cover the seat and the back of the couch with pink leaves or rose petals for color, pussy willows or moss for fluffiness, herb leaves for texture and fragrance, or any other kind of material you would like. You can make the cushion for the seat one large rectangular pillow, stuffing it with cotton fill then gluing or sewing it together. Make one for the seat and one for the back, if you would like. You can even glue on little ribbons to tie the seat to the back.

5 Decorate your couch or loveseat. You might intertwine interesting, tiny, dark roots into the top of the couch to give it an earthy look, as if it had been in a forest for many years. You could attach delicate, thin, gold metal coiled into a circle to the arms of the loveseat.

Your enchanting couch is now ready for all the intimate and happy conversations of your Neitherland companions.

The little gnome worked happily at his stove baking bread, hoping that the comforting aroma might encourage good deeds from his forest friends.

The Gnome's Woodstove and Sink

Making a Gnome's Woodstove

To make a heartwarming little stove, you will need some bark. We have found that cherry bark is one of the best types of bark to use. Birch and palm bark are also good materials to use to make a little stove or other similar pieces. Depending on where you live, you may be able to find even more unique kinds of bark or other similar materials.

YOU'LL NEED:

A Bark for the sides of the oven and shelves

B Cardboard for structure

C Four pieces of driftwood or small branches, stones, or shells for legs

D Kelp, different colored bark, or thick leaf for the stove burners

E Moss

1 Make a box shape from thin cardboard. Cut out six cardboard squares, each roughly 2 inches by 2 inches. Glue the pieces together to make a box the size you would like the oven to be.

2 Cut pieces of cherry or other bark to match the size of the cardboard box you have made. If you hold a piece of bark up to each side of the oven box, you will be able to measure what size to cut the bark.

Glue the pieces of bark onto the cardboard. Cover all the glue with moss. If you would prefer to skip using cardboard entirely, you can do so, using only bark to make the box.

3 Make the legs for the stove. Pick out interesting driftwood, branches, twigs, or even shells or stones to glue onto the bottom of the stove. Look for unique pieces to use, something that will give the stove charm and a sturdy look. Glue the legs onto the stove, and cover the glue with moss.

4 Make the back of the stove (similar to an old wood-burning cookstove) by cutting a piece of cardboard that is the width of the oven and about twice as tall.

To make a shelf, cut another small piece of cardboard the width of the stove but not very tall. For example, if you made the stove 2 inches wide, this piece should be about 2 inches by 3/4 inch. Cover this with bark.

5   Glue the small piece of cardboard or bark to the top of the stove back to make a shelf over the burners. Use small twigs or tendrils as braces to make the shelf more secure.

Glue the back of the stove, with its shelf, onto the back part of the oven, and cover all the visible cardboard with bark. Remember to add moss over the glue.

6   To make the four burners for the stove, it is best to choose a material that is a different color than the bark so the burners will be more visible. Kelp or a thick green leaf work well. Using scissors, cut tiny circles for the burners out of whatever material you choose, and glue these onto the top of the stove.

7   Decorate your stove however you would like. Make pots and pans from eucalyptus, acorn or any other kinds of pods; even tiny, round shells (that have a somewhat bowl-like shape will work). Add handles to the pots and pans by attaching a tiny branch or twig. You can glue the pots and pans onto the burners or just have them sitting on the stove.

We have made stovepipes for our stoves, which works wonderfully when you include your stove in the little Forest Cottage (on page 97). This part might need to be added after your cottage is constructed so you can see where to put the stovepipe. For example, in our Fairy Treehouse, the little stove in the kitchen has a stovepipe attached to it, and it comes out through the wall next to the stove (which is an outside wall). When you set your little stove into the Forest Cottage, it will definitely feel more like a real and usable piece for your woodland characters.

Making a Gnome's Sink

This is a stand-alone sink. You could also make the same type of sink for the bathroom of the Forest Cottage if you would like, but you may want to attach a little shelf or open cabinet for a bathroom sink. Of course, the best material to use for a sink is a shell, but there are other things you can use just as well, such as hollowed-out and dried oranges, limes, lemons, or avocados. These materials can be used for a sink as well as a bathtub and other similar shapes. For all of these, it is a good idea to fill the hollowed out fruit with rocks or beans to help it keep its shape while drying.

YOU'LL NEED:

A   Shell for the bowl of the sink

B   Shell or oblong pod for the support piece of the sink

C   Branch or piece of driftwood for the stand

D   Rocks to make a base

E   Tendrils for the faucet and handles

F   Moss

Tiny, round shell for a soap dish (not pictured)

1   Glue the shell that will be the bowl of the sink onto the shell or pod you've chosen for the support piece. Then glue these to the driftwood sink stand.

2   Glue rocks to the sink stand for the base. Use moss to strengthen the adhesive bond as well as cover any exposed glue.

3   Prepare the faucets and the handles of the sink. Cut a grapevine tendril that is curved for the faucet. It should be small enough that it fits with the size of the sink. Then cut two smaller tendrils for the handles. If you have some tiny pods or shells that look like they would work for the faucet and the handles, those can be used instead.

4   Glue the faucet and handle tendrils to the sink edge. Use moss to strengthen the adhesive bond as well as to cover any exposed glue.

5   Make a soap dish out of a tiny, round, open shell. Glue it down onto the edge of the sink. Cut a tiny piece of real soap and glue it to the sink bowl.

6   Cover any remaining glued areas with moss so your sink looks more natural. As an alternative, you could cover the glue with tiny shells if you would like or even small pieces of kelp, seaweed, or other materials from the ocean.

If you've made a sink for a kitchen, you could put tiny half shells (open shells that look like bowls) in the sink, as if a little fairy or elf were about to wash their dishes.

To create a little bathtub for the bathroom of your Forest Cottage, follow the same instructions for making the sink, but, of course, the shell you would use would be larger and perhaps a little longer. You could use an abalone shell for the bathtub or another type of shell. Glue on little stones or other shells for the feet, and make the faucet and handles again out of grapevine tendrils. Decorate your little bathtub any way you would like. To make it more interesting, try covering the outside of the bathtub with tiny shells, coral pieces, shiny stones, or even small pieces of driftwood.

A house is not a home
without the magic of music.

The Elfin King's Ancient Forest Piano

T he piano is a magical, wonderful instrument; it has a beautiful sound and the ability to evoke emotion and memories when played with sensitivity. This is an elaborate piece and will take time, but each step is quite interesting and you should find the materials fascinating to use. Part of the basic frame of the piano is made from dried eggplant skins, so you will first need to get some fresh eggplant to dry.

YOU'LL NEED:

A Dried skins of two eggplants for the sides and front of the piano

B Caplet of an eggplant or a pod for a lampshade

C Cardboard for the framework of the piano

D Foam board for the base of the keyboard

E Antique sheet music for the back of the piano and a book of music

F Dried onion skins or bark for the sides and front of the piano

G Tendrils or vines for braces and the lamp stand

H Capiz shells for the white keys

I Kelp, bark, or dark leather for the black keys

J Bark or driftwood for the seat of the bench and short branches for the legs

K Pods, seeds, shells, stones, flowers, and moss for decoration

Dark purple acrylic paint and a paintbrush (not pictured)

1   Cut the outer skins of the eggplant off, making the strips as long as possible. Try to use all of the outer skin, because the pieces shrink a little when they dry.

Save the caplet—the starlike part at the end of the eggplant that the stem was attached to. You can use this for the lamp on the piano. Cut the caplet away from the eggplant and carefully hollow it out to leave an open, empty space inside.

Follow the instructions for drying with borax on page 28. Set the eggplant pieces down into the borax mixture with the purple side up, and pour the mixture over them. Place the caplet in the mixture with the open side up; pour the borax mixture into the caplet so it will hold its bell-like shape. Be sure all the eggplant material is spaced apart so it will dry better. It will probably take about five days for the eggplant to dry; in the meantime, start making the frame of the piano.

2   Cut out two pieces of cardboard, each 6 inches by 6 inches. These will be the front and back pieces of the piano frame. Next, cut out four pieces, each 6 inches by 1 1/2 inches. These will be used as the sides, top, and bottom of the piano frame. The cardboard you use for the bottom of the piano should be a little thicker than the rest of the cardboard so that the piano stands up well. Glue all of these pieces together to make an enclosed box. Cover the glue with moss to strengthen the seams.

3   Paint all of the cardboard pieces a dark purple color so they don't show.

4   Cover the back of the piano with a beautiful sheet of antique music. If you don't have any old music, you can photocopy a page from a book of music onto paper that is textured and has an antique look to it. Cover the edges of the music with moss all the way around.

5   Cover the sides of the piano with bark, but only down to about an inch from the bottom. The lower part can be covered with the dried eggplant skin.

6   When the eggplant and caplet are completely dry, remove them carefully from the drying mixture. Dust all of the borax mixture from the eggplant skins, and clean the skins gently with a damp cloth.

Glue the eggplant pieces to the front of the piano and along the bottom inch of the sides. If you need to trim the pieces to fit them onto the piano, cut them carefully with scissors. Overlap each piece of eggplant to cover the cardboard and give the eggplant a layered look.

We recommend that you start with the front of the piano, beginning at the top right-hand corner. Glue the first piece of eggplant skin down onto the cardboard, making sure to use enough glue so the eggplant will attach well, then add another piece beside the first, overlapping it slightly. It is fine if the pieces curl up a little, but you don't want the cardboard to show at all.

7 Continue gluing the eggplant pieces onto the cardboard front, using the glue liberally and making sure all of the edges are attached well.

8 Add bark just below the keyboard to break up the eggplant and to help support the keyboard piece.

9 Glue eggplant pieces below the bark, as you did with the top part of the piano.

10 You can add small pieces of dried purple onion skins where the bark and the lower eggplant pieces join to cover the abrupt edge and to give another color to the piano. You can also use old leather, lichen, leaves, or whatever you would like.

11

Glue the last pieces of eggplant to the top and lower sides of the box.

12

For the keyboard, use a long, rectangular piece of foam board. It should be a little less than the width of the piano and about 1 1/4 inches deep. Foam board works well for the base of the keyboard since it is the right thickness. Glue the foam board just above the bark on the front of the piano, using the glue liberally so it attaches well; make sure it looks level.

It is a good idea to paint the underside of the foam board dark purple so the white doesn't show.

13

Add the legs and braces next. This will help support the keyboard. Choose branches for the legs that are somewhat thick, because they will need to be sturdy enough to hold up the keyboard and keep the rest of the piano level when it is completed. Cut them to the appropriate height to support the keyboard—ours were roughly 3 1/2 inches tall.

Glue these branches to the bottom of the foam board, just slightly in from each corner; use the glue liberally so this area will be sturdy.

Add braces from the legs to the lower part of the piano; choosing curvy branches or seaweed can make a better design. You can also add smaller, curvy branches for bracing just under the keyboard as well.

14 Add the actual piano keys. These are truly the most important part of the piano and will probably be what people see first when they look at this piece. We have used round capiz shells to make the piano keys. These are beautiful, sheer shells with a lovely, pearly look. They also cut very easily, which makes them a perfect material for the piano keys. You may need about three to four shells, since they are round and the curved edges may not work to make the straight-edged keys.

Measure the foam board to see how long to cut the shell pieces. We made our foam board about 1 1/4 inches deep, but it is best to see what size you will need for your keyboard because it may be different. Cut the shell pieces in long, rectangular shapes, making them all about the same width. Then glue them, one by one, onto the foam board, starting at one end and working all the way across to the other side of the piano. Try to make sure the front of the keys go all the way to the edge of the foam board.

15 Next, cut more shells into very small, almost squared pieces the same width as the keys you have just made, then glue them onto the foam board in front of each key. Use the glue sparingly so it won't show. Try to match up the front shells with the longer shells behind them, so it looks like they are one entire key.

Using a black fine-point pen, you can draw delicate lines in between each key to accentuate the white color of the keys.

16 To make the black piano keys, use flat pieces of black seaweed, dark-colored bark, or old, dark leather. You could paint any of these materials, if they are not dark enough, using thick, black acrylic paint. Cut small, rectangular shapes from the material you've chosen. Glue the black keys down onto the white keys at intervals of two and three.

17 Add a charming little lamp above the keyboard by using the eggplant caplet you dried earlier. To do this, glue the caplet to a piece of seaweed or kelp, a branch, or an interesting vine, then attach your finished lamp to the piano next to the keyboard. Use the glue liberally, and cover it with moss or lichen.

18 Add a cute little book of music above the keyboard. Using dried purple onion skins, make a picture frame shape, leaving a space in the middle for the music.

Cut out tiny sheets of handwritten or photocopied music and glue them together into the picture frame. It should look like a little book of music.

19 Add the little foot pedals at the bottom of the piano by gluing on three small rectangular pieces of bark, rounding the front edges a little with scissors.

20 Finally, add moss and decorate the piano. Use moss in areas that need softening or a little more texture. You can cut the eggplant at the top of the piano into scallop shapes and decorate different areas with seaweed, kelp, tiny shells, and pods. Use star anise seed pods, dried scabiosa flowerets, tiny pieces of coral, and small stones.

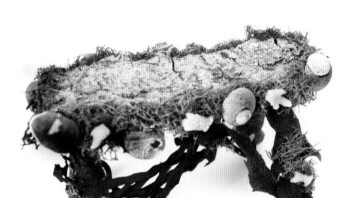

21 The last step in creating your Elfin King's Piano is to make the little piano bench. The design for this piece is very similar to the table you have already made (see A Fairy Table on page 43), except that you would want to make it short enough to fit under the piano keyboard. Cut out a rectangular piece of bark for the top of the bench, and use branches that match the legs of the piano.

Measure how high to make the bench, then cut the branches for the legs accordingly.

Glue the legs to the underside of the bark seat at each corner, and add braces to keep it sturdy.

Add moss to cover the glue and decorate the piano bench with seaweed fronds, shells, and coral.

Now your piano is ready for the musically inclined elf to enjoy!

You will treasure the little
creations you make and
bring to life with your
wonderful artistry!

The Forest Cottage

with Accessories

A s you make your beautiful Forest Cottage or Fairy House, use your imagination, and try to make something that has never been created before. You will, at last, have a charming little house for all the lovely furniture pieces you've made! Consider leaving enough space outside the cottage for a little garden.

YOU'LL NEED:

A   Hot glue, carpenter's glue, and household glue

B   Hammer and chisel

C   Modeling clay, brown and gray acrylic paint, and small paintbrush

D   Cardboard for templates

E   Square piece of plywood for the base

F   Driftwood, branches, wood, and shingles for the walls, roof, and doorframe

G   Small pieces of leather for the door hinges

H   Thin wire for door handles

I   Mica for windows

J   Moss, pods, flowers, herb leaves, etc. for covering glue and decorating

1 PREPARING THE PIECES

Prepare the base for your cottage and choose the materials you would like to use for the walls. We've used plywood for the base and weathered shingles for the walls in the cottage we've made here. You can also frame your house completely with driftwood and fill it in with whatever materials you have. If you decide to use shingles, bark, or cardboard templates, cut them to the size you would like for the walls.

WINDOW OPENINGS

To make a window space out of a shingle or a piece of wood, use a small saw and a chisel. You can also make a separate square window frame and glue the pieces of the frame together. Glue the frame between two wall pieced, then just fill in above and below the window with smaller pieces of wood.

PUTTING THE WALLS TOGETHER

Temporarily glue the wood for each of the walls onto the base without attaching them permanently in place by just using enough glue here and there to tack the pieces down. That way, you can see where you want the windows and doors to be and how many pieces of wood you will need.

Then, after you've chosen the layout of your pieces, use a liberal amount of glue to attach everything together securely. Notice that we added wooden trim on all sides of the plywood base, as well—this is optional. You can just paint it brown or green and embellish it with moss, if you'd prefer.

With all of the walls up, the back is left open, and the two front walls are angled toward the door so it is not a perfect square. There is also an opening for the double door in the front.

2   Use modeling clay to fill in the seams where the windows were put in. If you have a piece of wood that you really want to use but it is not quite the right size or has a gap in it, modeling clay can be used to fill it in. Modeling clay also works well to mend a piece of wood if it cracks.

3   Close the opening over the doorway with a piece of wood glued to the two parts of the front wall. Cut out a half-circle notch so the door can be rounded at the top. By doing this now, you will have a temporary brace to rest the roof on before you put in the door.

4   Glue the two roof pieces nearest the door to the outside walls, one at a time. Use a piece of cardboard or wood as a brace to hold up the first roof piece while the glue sets. It is not necessary to glue the brace in place permanently—just use it until the two roof pieces are glued together.

Glue the rest of the roof pieces the same way. To brace the other roof pieces, use a longer branch placed inside the house from the floor up to the roof. Where these two meet, just overlap one on top of the other and glue them together. Repeat this process until you have the whole roof covered. Apply wood glue to the inside and outside of all the roof joints and let them dry overnight. Then add moss over all the roof joints.

You can adjust how much the roof projects out over the base with changes to the bracing piece.

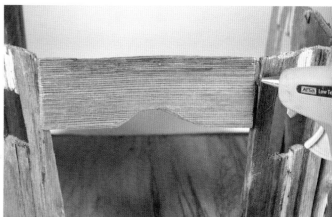

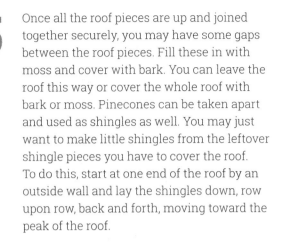

5 Once all the roof pieces are up and joined together securely, you may have some gaps between the roof pieces. Fill these in with moss and cover with bark. You can leave the roof this way or cover the whole roof with bark or moss. Pinecones can be taken apart and used as shingles as well. You may just want to make little shingles from the leftover shingle pieces you have to cover the roof. To do this, start at one end of the roof by an outside wall and lay the shingles down, row upon row, back and forth, moving toward the peak of the roof.

Leaves can also be layered onto the roof, overlapped in an interesting way. A kind of thatched roof can be made by cutting wild grasses and gluing them down into overlapping, shingle-style rows. You would need to start at the bottom and work your way up so you can overlap the materials you are using.

6 Once the roof is done and you've covered all the glue with moss, you can cut pieces for the front door. Frame the doors with branches to add more variety to your design. Then make little brass door pulls out of wire and glue them on, covering the glue with moss.

7 To attach the doors, make hinges using thin strips of leather. Glue one end of the leather strip to the door and loop the other end around the post and back towards the door. Glue this end to the back of the door to make a complete loop that the door can swing on.

8   If you have gaps in your door, use little pieces of bark to cover the corners above the door. These will add texture and uniqueness to the overall house.

9   Use more modeling clay to fill in any remaining gaps in the structure of your cottage. Roll out a small amount of the modeling clay in the palm of your hand. Then push it into the gaps, smooth it out with your fingers, and let it dry. When the clay has dried completely, paint over it with a mixture of brown, green, and gray acrylic paint so that it resembles the color of the shingles. If you are using a different kind of material for the walls, choose paint colors that will match the walls you have made. When the paint is dry, glue moss over the area.

10   To fill in the windows, you can use mica, an amazing mineral that looks just like glass. It is often found in large blocks that you can peel off into thin sheets. Take off a layer of the mica and cut it carefully with scissors, then glue it into the window area. You can then cut little wooden frames to glue over the edges of the mica and around your window. Add moss to the corners of the window, covering all the glue that is visible.

11 To make planter boxes for your cottage, you can split shingles or a piece of wood with a chisel or cut them with pruners. You will need three identical rectangular pieces of wood for the front, back, and bottom, and two identical square pieces for the sides.

Glue them together and then attach the boxes to the area right under the window. Be sure to add moss underneath the boxes and brace them as well, for more stability. Then fill your little window box with beautiful dried flowers, wild grasses, and herbs.

12 To finish, decorate your Forest Cottage. As in making other pieces, the embellishments can really bring the cottage to life. A cottage left plain and simple is fine, too, but adding pretty flowers and leaves, vines, tendrils, pods, shells, and stones can add interesting color and detail to your little forest house.

Now all that's left is to move into your charming little house! Set your little furniture, books, dishes, and everything else that you have made into your beautiful Forest Cottage. Your wonderful creations are all that is needed to make your cottage feel warm and bright and cozy.

As you move in, find out what else your fairy or elfin family might need. Make a little broom, tiny plates, an ironing board and iron, and a mailbox. You could even make little rugs for the floors by braiding vines and weaving them together or using cattail down and soft moss on the floor to cushion the little elves' feet. And what about the outside? Make a wheelbarrow, a mailbox, and a watering can.

Outdoor Accessories

A MAILBOX

YOU'LL NEED:

A   Piece of curled of bark or thin cardboard for the body of the mailbox

B   Small piece of bark for the lid of the mailbox

C   Driftwood, a branch, or a root for the post

D   Stone for the base

E   Tendril and a small, red flower for the mailbox flag

F   Paper to make letters and a newspaper

G   Moss to cover the glue and decorate

1   Find a piece of curled cherry bark to use for the main part of the mailbox where the mail will go. You could also use cardboard, bend it into a cylinder shape, and cover it with bark.

2   Cut two U-shaped pieces of bark for the door and the back of the mailbox. Glue one piece of bark to the back of the box. Glue the second piece of bark to the front so that the mailbox will look open. Cover the glue with moss.

3   Glue the mailbox to the top of a thick piece of driftwood, a root, or a branch, using lots of glue and moss. Then glue the mailbox post between two or three rocks that will have enough weight to hold the mailbox upright.

4   On one side of the mailbox, attach a tendril for the flag and glue a small, red flower on the end. Cover all the visible glue with moss.

5   Decorate your mailbox, and fill it with a small roll of newspaper or little envelopes with letters.

A WHEELBARROW WITH FLOWERS

YOU'LL NEED:

A Cardboard for templates

B Bark to cover the sides and make the wheel

C Twigs for the handles and legs

D Flowers to fill the wheelbarrow

1 Cut out templates for the five sides of the wheelbarrow. The bottom and side pieces should be basically rectangular but are wider in the back and narrower in the front. The back and front pieces are square shapes, the back being larger than the front.

2 After cutting out the template shapes, glue them together to make the basic frame of the wheelbarrow. Then add moss to strengthen the seams.

Cut pieces of bark to match the framework pieces of the wheelbarrow.

3 Glue the bark pieces to the outside of the cardboard frame. Glue two branches, pods, or tendrils to the back piece of the wheelbarrow to make the handles. Add moss over the glue.

To make the legs, cut two thin pieces of bark and fold them in the middle to form a triangular shape. Glue the ends underneath the back part of the wheelbarrow and add moss.

4 You can make your own wheel for the wheelbarrow by cutting a small circle out of bark or a thin piece of driftwood. Use an awl or nail to puncture a small hole in the middle for the axle. Or you can buy a wooden or metal wheel from a craft store.

5 To attach the wheel, cut two small branches of the same length for the axle and a third, smaller branch that will fit through the hole in the wheel. Use the fourth branch under the wheelbarrow, joining the axles.

6 Glue one end of each of the two longer branches to the bottom of the wheelbarrow and cover with moss. Put the smaller branch through the wheel and attach the ends to the two axle branches at the front. Glue the last branch onto the axles for support. Put moss over all of the glue and remove any glue strings. Make sure the wheel will turn properly and the wheelbarrow stands well.

7 Fill the little wheelbarrow with flowers, wild grasses, and herbs. You can also make some little gardening tools and set them in the wheelbarrow.

Make a rake and a watering can to go with your wheelbarrow.

A RAKE

For the rake, glue a small rectangular piece of bark onto the end of a sturdy branch. Then, glue six or seven tiny twigs onto the end of the bark for the prongs of the rake.

A WATERING CAN

Make a watering can from thin cardboard cut into a cylinder shape, enclosed on one end. Cover this with a leaf; use a tendril for a handle and a long, curved pod for the spout.

You'll make a face of clay and arms of wood, clothe him in moss, and crown him with an acorn pod, but you breathe life into a woodland character when you pour love and inspiration into your creation.

Woodland Characters

Creating fairytale characters for your houses and cottages can be wonderfully fun, and you can make some amazing little people, just five or six inches tall. Once you gain confidence, the possibilities are endless; you can truly be inventive.

YOU'LL NEED:

Twigs, branches, small pieces of driftwood, pods, pinecones, or kelp bulbs for the basic body

Poppy pods, acorns, sea onions, or clay for the head, hats, and pouches

Seeds and tiny berries for eyes and other features

Twigs, driftwood, or roots for arms and legs

Clay or pods for making hands, feet, and shoes

Lamb's wool, flower petals, or seaweed for hair

Palm bark, herbs, leaves, lichen, moss, or hand-made paper for clothes

Flowers, leaves, herbs, seeds, berries, pods, and paint for decorating and adding details

Fine-point marking or felt pen to draw faces

Helpful Hint: You can also refer to Appendix A on page 170 for photos of other materials to use for your characters.

TORSO

Choose materials for the torso, legs, and arms of your character from the list of materials above. Use a mixture of different materials.

Pick branches that have bends and curves at the appropriate places for elbows, hips, and knees to make your character's posture look natural. If you are making a paper or cloth person, add jointed arms and legs.

BASE

Mounting your characters on some kind of base will help them look more finished and is also good for characters that might not be stable enough to stand on their own. There are many objects that can be used for bases that will be in keeping with an all-natural setting. You could mount a little person on a small piece of driftwood or have them sit in a swing; they could be walking on a giant sunflower or a shiny stone. You can also mount them on a dried orange, a large shell, or a pinecone.

HEADS

Make the head for your character. The easiest way to make the head and face for any kind of woodland or fairyland character is to use poppy pods or acorns. Kelp bulbs also work well, since they have natural hair. Pinecones or anything with a round or oval shape work well, too.

FACES

A face can be painted onto a clay head or you can glue on tiny beads or pictures of eyes, noses, and other features for a face.

HAIR

Glue hair to the top of the head, using seaweed, kelp strands, wild grass, strawflower fluff, lamb's wool, or doll's hair.

HATS

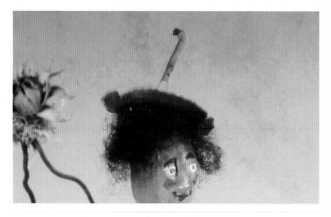

Attach a bell-shaped pod or flower for a hat. Decorate it with tiny flowers or shells.

HANDS

Hands and feet can be formed from clay or cut from softened seaweed or kelp and glued onto a twig arm.

SHOES

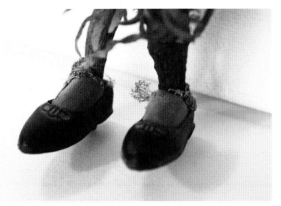 

Hakea pods, bark, shells, stones, old doll shoes, or papier-mâché can be used to make shoes.

CLOTHING

Add clothing to your characters; moss, soft and velvety herb leaves, and pretty flowers make wonderful little clothes for elves and fairies. We have also used old fabric, photos, palm bark, tree bark, moss, lichen, and leaves to make coats with pod buttons, vests, and other amazing clothes.

DECORATIONS

 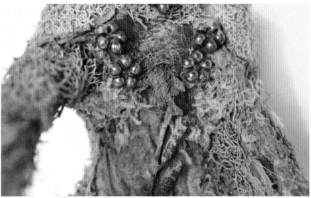

Finally, decorate your little person with flowers, moss, leaves, and tiny shells. Give them accessories: a book, a broom, an instrument, a lantern, or a butterfly net.

I hear the voices of nature, and age slips away, stories unfold, and time is only a word. I create with nature because I see the beauty of the world. I know it is a beautiful and endless garden.

The Fairy Garden

There are many different ways to create a fairy garden. The basic idea of any fairy garden would be the same, though, for any project; it would be centered on the fairytale quality of an enchanted world, one that has a magical, childlike feeling about it and has your own wonderful creativity shining through it.

A Large piece of cardboard or wood for the base

B Moss for the lawn

C Twigs, branches, vines, and tendrils for the fence

D Branches, vines, or coated wire for the archway

E Stones for the path

F Curved pods or bark to cover the outside edges of the garden

G Flowers and herbs for the garden

H Small pods or acorn caps to decorate the fence

1 Using the thick piece of cardboard or wood (which could be fiberboard or plywood), cut the base into a circle or a square. Paint the base green with acrylic paint, let it dry, then cover it with moss. Start in one corner and work toward the other end of the base, filling it in from left to right as you go and making sure to lay the moss down thick enough that it looks lush and fluffy without any gaps revealing the cardboard or wood.

2 Decide what kinds of pieces you would like to include in your garden before you create a path, flowerbed, or fence. You could include a little chair; a table with paints, brushes, and an easel; a wishing well; a tower; a swing; a fountain; a birdbath; a dovecote; a little bridge over a pond; a little gazebo; a harp; wind chimes; or any other garden objects. In our example, we chose to include a wishing well, which you will learn to make on page 129.

With your design laid out, make the little stone path. Start at one edge of the base and glue the little stones down in a narrow pattern, ending at the point where you will add the wishing well, tower, or other piece. Try to set the stones as close together as you can, adding moss, lichen, or little flowers in between the stones if there are any empty spaces.

Create a little twig wattle fence along the path (see step 4) or just let it meander along by itself.

3 Make a flower bed by gluing rows of different dried flowers along in one corner in a roughly rectangular shape. We used purple statice, golden yarrow, larkspur, baby's breath, and little hydrangeas. In between the rows of flowers, add brown or chartreuse moss to serve as soil.

4 Make a tiny wattle fence for the flower bed by weaving wild strawberry vines together around the flower garden, leaving the area near the path open so that a little fairy or elf could walk into their lovely flower patch.

5 Create some kind of trim around the base of your fairy garden. We have used large pods here to cover the edge of our base. Any kind of pod will work, or you could add pinecones, bark, shells, or little stones.

Next, make the wattle fence that will surround the entire fairy garden. Glue a sturdy branch down into the moss near the edge of the base and to the left of the stone path. Be sure to add a good amount of moss to the base of the first twig so it will be a strong post for the fence. From there, glue down the same kinds of twigs all along the edge of the base, spacing them about 2–3 inches apart. You should end up with the final branch (or post for the fence) just to the right of the stone path, leaving the front part of the stone path open for an archway door.

6 Weave branches or vines onto the little branch posts around the edge of your fairy garden base. Flexible vines or branches would work best for this part of the fence, such as long willow branches, green grapevines, or wisteria vines. Start at the first post on the left of the stone path, gluing one end of the vine onto the post branch and securing it with moss. Then weave it behind the next post and in front of the one after that, each time going either behind the post or in front of it, alternating each time. Continue on until you reach the end of the vine or branch you are weaving with, then glue that end to the nearest post and cover the glue with moss.

7 Repeat this with more vines until the fence is filled out. If the vine you are using doesn't quite reach the next post, just tuck it into the nearest vine, gluing it and mossing it well.

8 Glue a pod or acorn cap to the very top of each post.

9 To form the basic shape of the archway, it is best to create it separately and then attach it to the fairy garden. Use coated wire branches (we found ours at Michaels craft store) or another kind of thick, flexible vine. You could also use three or four vines and weave them together to make the archway. Bend the coated wire branch into an upside-down U to make the basic frame.

Glue more vines around the frame of the archway until it looks finished. Then glue the ends of it onto the base of the fairy garden at each side of the fence, using the glue liberally and covering the glue with moss. You can brace the archway door to the fence with other little branches as well to make it sturdier.

10 Decorate the archway, the fence, and the flower garden. Try out different materials, use lots of color, and make this creation as beautiful as you can imagine. When it is all finished, you can add other pieces—like the wheelbarrow, watering can, and mailbox—to make your fairy garden complete.

LIVING FAIRY GARDEN

You could also consider making a "living" fairy garden. Grow real plants within the garden! It would take a little research and planning, but it would be ever-changing and beautiful. To do this, find a deep enough planter or container to hold soil with good drainage. Rather than covering the floor of the fairy garden base with moss, you could plant herbal ground covers, such as creeping thyme, aromatic thyme, Corsican mint, Roman chamomile, creeping rosemary, or oregano. These are very low-growing herbal plants that have wonderful fragrances and can be pruned short to look like a lawn. If you mix several varieties, the base or "lawn" of your fairy garden will look and smell even more wonderful and should have little flowers growing amongst the other herbs. For the little flower patch inside the fairy garden, plant tiny flowers or herbs. If you used taller branches for the fence, you could plant vining flowers to grow up the branches.

This type of fairy garden would obviously take much more time to maintain but would surely bring many hours of beauty and enjoyment. With real, living plants, flowers, and herbs, you would surely attract many curious fairies and elves, who would probably never want to leave such a wonderful, miniature paradise!

Come with us to sit amid giant yellow
flowers, sip chamomile tea, and listen to
enchanted stories of fairyland.

The Elfin Tea Party

with Accessories

We usually make The Elfin Tea Party from grapevine branches, as we will do in the following instructions. The Elfin Tea Party includes chairs, a table with an umbrella, and tiny teatime accessories.

Making Elfin Tea Party Chairs

YOU'LL NEED (PER CHAIR):

A   Two 6-inch branches for the back legs and the back of the chair

B   Two shorter branches for the front legs

C   Square of branches or a piece of bark for the seat

D   Four to six decorative vines or tendrils for the rungs and backs of the chairs

E   Leaf skeleton pieces for the back of the chair

F   Moss, flowers, lichen, and shells for decoration

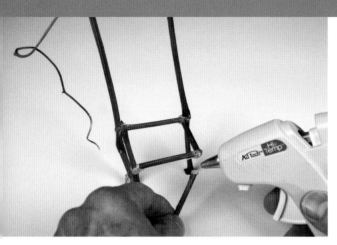

1 Make the base of a chair using steps 1–4 for A Little Chair on page 38. However, instead of using four short, even branches for the legs, this chair will require using two short branches for the front legs and two long branches that will serve as the back legs and chair back (as shown).

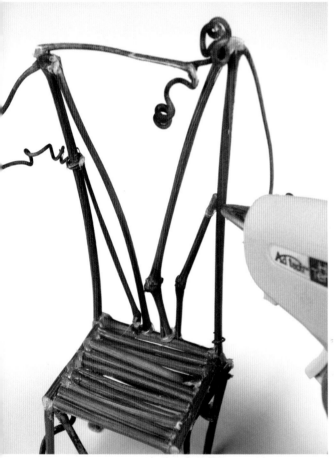

2 For the back of the chair, you can use a solid piece of bark, or you can make a more whimsical design. Cut two branches to 3 1/2 inches and two to 2 1/2 inches. If you have made a smaller or larger chair, you can just hold the branches up to your chair and see what length you will need for the back of the chair.

Glue the longest two branches or vines into a V shape, attaching them at each end to the inner frame of the chair back. Cut the ends of the branches at an angle, as in the photo, to help them fit into the back more easily.

Glue the next two branches alongside the first two, creating a shorter V outside the first. You can use more or fewer branches in this pattern to create a sturdy backrest.

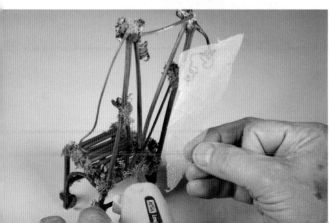

3 Consider gluing something between the branches. We often cut a leaf skeleton to go into the V shape in the back.

4 Make another chair similar to the first, then decorate your chairs and embellish them in the style you want. In addition to using leaf skeletons for the chair backs, you can add larkspur flowers, tendrils, and moss to decorate the chairs.

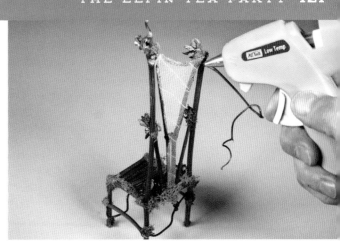

Making a Tea Table

Your table should be wide enough (or long enough, if you want to make a rectangular table) to accommodate an umbrella stand attached at the center of the table, two chairs (or more) at the sides of the table, and little dishes or teacups on the tabletop. In these instructions, we will make our table four inches by four inches.

YOU'LL NEED:

A   Square of branches, 4 inches by 4 inches, or a square piece of bark for the tabletop

B   Four straight branches for the legs, each roughly 3 1/2 inches long

C   Eight small tendrils or twigs for braces

D   Moss

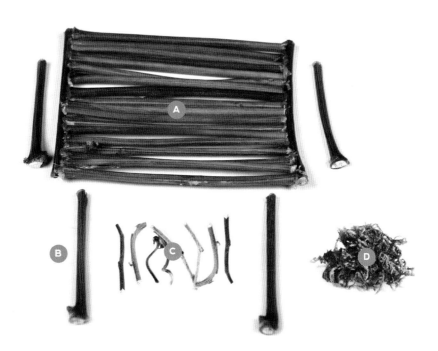

1   Make a table using steps 1–4 for A Fairy Table on page 44.

In this example, we've made the tabletop out of a 4-by-4-inch square of branches.

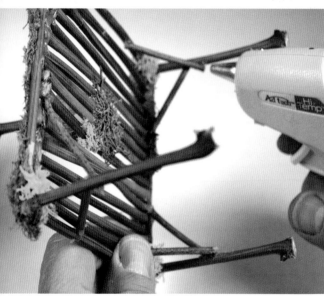

2   You will definitely need to brace the table, but you do not want the braces to get in the way of sliding chairs under the table. It is best to attach small braces in the corners of the table. Do this by gluing a small brace an inch from the top of the table leg to the tabletop, roughly an inch away from the corner. Use two braces for each leg, with plenty of glue and moss for stability. You can also glue braces from the lower part of the legs up to the center of the underside of the table. Neither of these kinds of braces should get in the way of the chairs fitting underneath the table.

Making the Umbrella

YOU'LL NEED:

A One branch, 3 1/2–4 1/2 inches long, for the umbrella stand

B Eucalyptus pod for the base of the umbrella stand

C Small cardboard pot pie container for the frame of the umbrella

D Paintbrush and brown acrylic paint (or another suitable color) to cover the container

E Pods, bark, and tendrils for dishes and decoration

F Moss, hydrangea and larkspur flowers, and rose buds for decoration of the umbrella

G Three or four smaller branches for braces

1 To make the canopy of the umbrella, start with a cardboard pot pie container (perhaps an odd thing to use, but it actually works perfectly for this). This bowl shape will be used as the base for all the beautiful flowers on the umbrella. Wash and dry the container well, then paint it the same color as the flowers will be (just using normal acrylic paint) and let the paint dry. Alternatively, you could also use a beautiful, thick leaf.

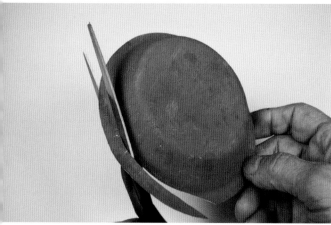

2 Trim the ends of the painted pie container so it won't be quite so wide. If you are making an Elfin Tea Party set that is larger, perhaps you would not need to trim the container and could just leave it the size it is.

3 Next, decorate the cardboard canopy base with dried or silk hydrangea flowers. Other flowers that work beautifully are tiny roses, larkspur, dried delphinium, daisies, and cosmos. Starting at the top center of the cardboard frame, glue the flowers very close together so the umbrella will look thick and full. The cardboard canopy could also be covered with leaves; you could glue them together, overlapping them and adding a few flowers here and there.

When you have covered the entire surface of the top of the cardboard, set the umbrella aside for a moment as you prepare the table for the umbrella.

4   Glue a eucalyptus or gum tree pod to the middle of the top of the table. Add a good amount of glue and moss around the pod and even underneath the table where the pod is attached so it stays secure.

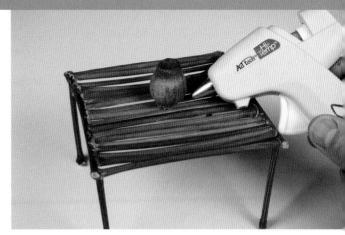

5   Prepare the umbrella stand by cutting a branch roughly 3 1/2–4 1/2 inches long. If your chairs are taller or shorter than in our example, adjust the height of the stand. The umbrella for the Tea Party set needs to be high enough to go over the tops of the chairs.

Glue the stand into the gum tree pod and liberally cover the glue with moss. Make sure the stand is attached securely inside the pod.

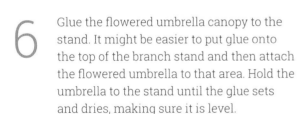

6   Glue the flowered umbrella canopy to the stand. It might be easier to put glue onto the top of the branch stand and then attach the flowered umbrella to that area. Hold the umbrella to the stand until the glue sets and dries, making sure it is level.

7   Brace the canopy of the umbrella by gluing four small twigs from the top of the stand to the four corners of the bottom of the canopy.

8 Be sure to add moss over any glue. Adding moss to the underside of the table where the pod is attached is a good idea, too.

If your umbrella is still unstable, try applying more glue and moss and holding the areas you are gluing until the glue has set. You can also wire the stand to the table—going around the base, under the table, and back up again to make it stronger—then glue and cover with moss.

Accessories

The accessories for the Elfin Tea Party are a teapot, teacups and saucers, little glasses and plates, a candle in a candle holder, and tiny foodstuffs. As you have already learned how to create a little teapot, teacup, and saucer for A Fairy Table on page 45, we will explain the other accessories here.

GLASSES AND PLATES

YOU'LL NEED:

A   Tall, tiny pods

B   Rounded pieces of bark, leaves, stones, or shells

1   Find a tiny pod that is tall enough to resemble a drinking glass; sometimes you can even decorate a pod with flowers or leaves to make it look like a glass.

2   Plates can just be made from rounded pieces of bark, leaves, or a tiny stone or shell. You could even draw little designs onto the plate or add pressed flowers.

A CANDLE AND CANDLE HOLDER

YOU'LL NEED:

A   Small, white birthday candle

B   Acorn cap or open pod for the holder

C   Grapevine tendril for the handle

D   Moss

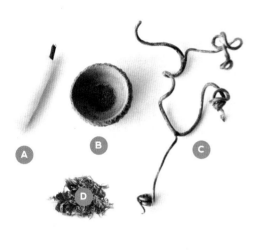

Candles can be used in any room in the house; they can even be attached to a wall, like a sconce. You can try and stretch your new skills by making a candelabra or chandelier.

1   Cut the candle down to about 1 inch tall.

2   Burn the candle down very slightly and drip wax into the acorn cap or pod so it looks like it has been used.

3   Glue the candle into the acorn cap.

4   Attach a grapevine tendril to the acorn cap for a handle.

5   Add moss to wherever there is glue showing, and add tiny flowers or shells..

TEA PARTY FOODSTUFFS

YOU'LL NEED: Various pods, seeds, berries, herbs, leaves, little stones, and shells

Imagine the most delightful little cakes, fruits, pastries, sandwiches, or other delicious foods. Using natural materials, you can create a wonderful summer party for your fairies and elves.

TINY CAKE

To make a tiny cake, you could cover a square shape of some kind (a pod or even a tiny box) with lamb's ear leaves or pussy willows (anything soft). Decorate the little cake with flowers. Embellish it to make it truly amazing!

BOWL OF FRUIT

Use tiny seeds, berries, pods, flower buds, rose hips, or other materials to resemble different kinds of fruit. Set them in tiny pods or open shells as bowls or put them on bits of bark for platters.

PASTRIES

Pastries could be similar to cakes; use your imagination and see what you can come up with. Herb leaves work wonderfully, especially scented ones that are fuzzy and soft. Combining these with flowers makes wondrous fairy pastries!

SANDWICHES

Put layers of different leaves together topped with tiny lilac flowerets to make tiny fairy sandwiches.

Nature has a way
of calming the spirit
and bringing to mind
remembrances of one's
childhood, that simple joy
and love of life that is a
natural part of looking
at the world as a child.

The Garden Wishing Well

The Wishing Well is a delightful piece to make and may bring back wonderful memories for you if you have ever been in an old-fashioned garden that had a lovely wishing well in one corner. There is something magical about this kind of piece, as it depicts older, simpler times.

YOU'LL NEED:

A Bark for the well, roof, and bucket

B Cylindrical carton or bottle for a well template

C Cardboard for bottom of the well

D Three branches for the roof support

E Flowers, tendrils, moss, and pods for decoration

1 Wrap a long piece of bark around a carton or bottle, and glue the ends of the bark together but not to the bottle. Once the bark frame holds its shape, you can remove the carton out from inside the bark.

If you do not have enough bark to go all the way around the form you are using, glue smaller pieces together to get the shape you want. We created our basic wishing well shape by using two pieces of bark and then gluing the edges together with other narrower strips of bark.

2 Glue a circular piece of cardboard onto the bottom of the well and cover any visible glue with moss. You can also use bark for the bottom of the well; use the piece of cardboard as a template to measure the right size for the bark piece.

Next, you will need to glue bark around the top edges of the wishing well to make a ledge all the way around it. This will help hold the round shape of the well together.

3   Glue two 7-inch branches to each end of a 3-inch branch. They will make a long, squared U shape.

Glue the open ends of the U-shaped brace to the bottom of the inside of the cylinder. Then, cover the glue with moss. This will provide support for the roof.

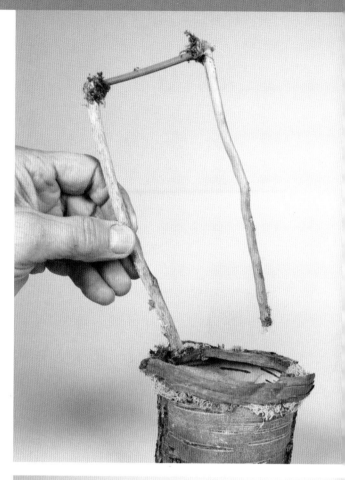

4   Glue two thick pieces of bark together, both at a slight angle to make a peaked roof. The bark should be wide enough to come out over the wishing well frame as a roof would. You can also add two small triangular pieces of bark to the front and back of the roof to join them together.

When the glue has set, securing the roof slats, use liberal amounts of glue to attach the roof to the top of the branch frame above the well. Use moss to strengthen the joints.

5 Make a small water bucket by shaping a thin piece of bark into a cylinder, gluing the sides together, and adding a round piece to the bottom.

Glue a grapevine tendril to the top sides of the bucket for a handle.

Attach the handle to the middle of the top support branch under the roof so the bucket will hang over the open part of the wishing well.

6 Add curled pieces of cherry bark on the ends and top of the roof, and decorate it with pods, tendrils, flowers, and even little stones.

You can even cut out different designs from a darker colored bark and glue them on as decoration.

The wishing well is a charming piece. It can reflect a time gone by—a period in our history when life was simple and farms were much more prevalent. Making your miniature fairyland wishing well will perhaps bring about even more enchanting feelings.

When you create by the work
of your hands, using nature
and seeing it up close, the
world doesn't seem so big
and ominous. It becomes
intriguing, like the stars.

Tower for the Elfin King

The Tower for the Elfin King is a rustic, charming, and earthy piece. It brings to mind childhood fairytales of hobbits and elves; it is a tribute to ancient architecture from a fairytale realm.

YOU'LL NEED:

A Cardboard for the walls, base, and roof of the tower

B Bark to cover the cardboard

C Modeling clay for the roof

D Paint brushes and acrylic paint (dark brown and forest green)

E Twigs and tendrils for the stairway

F Moss, lichen, and pods to decorate

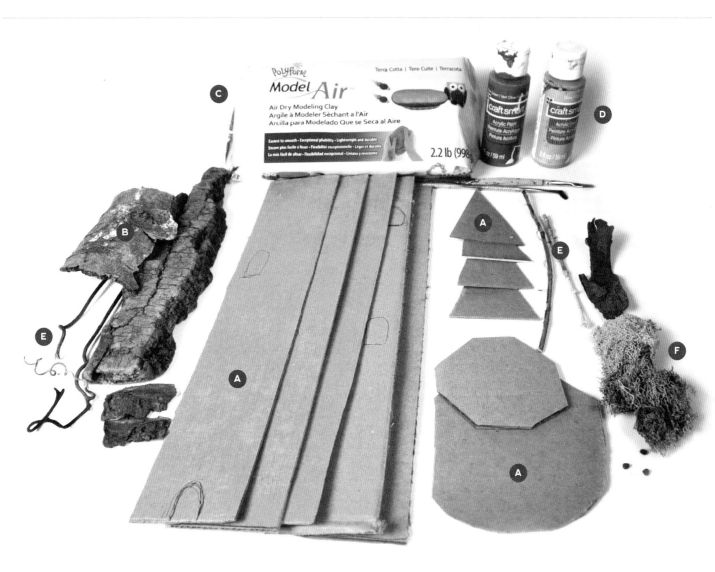

1   Cut out five sides of similar shapes from cardboard so that they are 11 inches tall and 2 inches wide.

Take time before you glue the walls together to decide where you want windows, doors, and balconies. Draw each out in pencil to make cutting easier.

Using an Exacto knife or scissors, cut out the windows for the walls. We made eight windows. Space them out in different areas of the tower.

You can also cut out the doorways now. We designed our tower to have a doorway on the bottom of the tower and one on the top.

Plan where you want the stairways, doors, and balconies before you glue the walls together.

2   Glue the five pieces of cardboard together. Use the glue liberally so that the walls will be sturdy.

3   Glue the tower onto a thick piece of cardboard to form a base. Trim away extra cardboard.

4 Turn the tower over, place it on a piece of cardboard, and trace around it. Cut out the traced piece of cardboard and glue it inside the open end of the tower about 1/4 inch down from the tops of the walls. You may need to trim it slightly for it to fit.

Cut out five identical cardboard triangles, each about 2 inches wide at the base (the same width as each of the walls). The height of the triangles is up to you; taller triangles will make a higher, more pointed roof.

Set the base of each triangle in the top of the tower, one triangle to each wall. Connect the tops of the triangles together in the center to form a five-sided peaked roof. Glue everything together securely.

5 Add layers of modeling clay onto the roof, pressing the clay down gently onto the cardboard. The clay will make the roof sturdier.

Add more modeling clay at the top of the tower by rolling the clay in your hand then pressing and smoothing it onto the pointed top of the roof. Curl the tip of the clay over slightly.

In a random pattern, make indentions into the modeling clay with a small tool or twig.

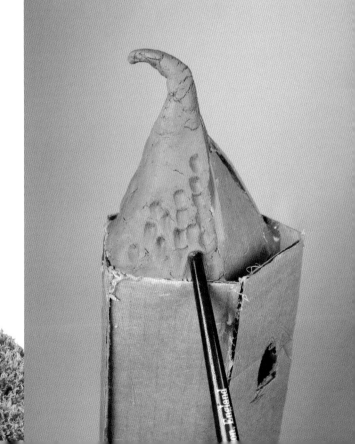

6 Paint the roof an earthy dark brown color, then go over it lightly with a little forest green.

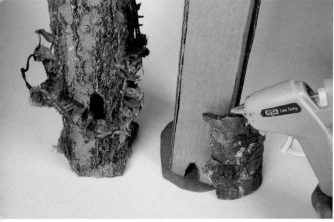

7 Glue bark to all of the exterior surfaces of the walls, leaving the windows open. It is easier to cut the windows and doors out from the bark before gluing it to the cardboard. Make the pattern and texture interesting. Be sure to cover up all the glue with plenty of moss.

8 When you have finished covering the tower with bark, glue small pieces of bark at the base of each window to make balconies. Cut the bark the same width as the window; it can extend out about a half inch to make it wide enough for a tiny elf to stand on.

9 You can also add small squares of bark around the top of the tower to form battlements.

10 Glue small twigs or tendrils that have a slight curve from one balcony to another to make stairs. Then add little pieces of bark for the steps in between the branches, and cover the glue with moss.

11 The final step is to add moss or lichen to any areas where the glue is showing and decorate the tower with pods, stones, dried herbs, and berries.

The Tower for the Elfin King has a wonderful storybook feeling about it. It would lend itself very well to a little play set in the forest, surrounded by lush green ferns and tiny fir trees just starting to grow. It is like an adventure to try to think of ways to utilize the natural creations you make and turn them into a wonderful, enchanted world full of surprises!

Making this little wagon is a step toward living in a more natural, rustic world.

The Gardener's Wagon

The wagon we have created here could be used for carrying moss to the garden to set about between the rows of flowers. A little wagon could be filled with gardener's tools or potted plants.

YOU'LL NEED:

A   Cardboard for the wagon body frame

B   Bark to cover the cardboard body

C   Four wheels made from bark or wood or from old toy cars

D   Small twigs for the spokes

E   Pods for wheel covers

F   Two branches for axels

G   Branch for the handle

H   Moss to cover glue and to fill the wagon

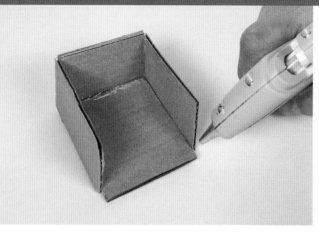

1 Create a basic box shape out of cardboard, leaving the top and front open.

2 Line the box shape with bark, inside and out. Or, if you would prefer, make the box out of bark without a cardboard frame.

3 At the front of the wagon, make a bench seat of smaller, similar kinds of bark and glue it into the open space rather than enclosing the box as in the back. Add another strip of bark for the driver's feet to rest on, gluing it below the bench and to the sides of the front of the wagon. Think of making two stair steps, one for the bench and another for the footrest.

Cover all the glued areas with moss to make the wagon stronger.

4 Glue a long branch onto the bottom of the front of the wagon, just below the footrest, to make a handle. You can add a few smaller branches at the opposite end of the handle to help pull the wagon.

5   Make four wheels from thick bark or a thinner cherry bark. You can also purchase four metal or wooden wheels and cover them with moss or leave them as they are to support your wagon. The wheels shown here were made totally from cherry bark. The little spokes were made from tiny twigs; the wheel covers are pods.

6   Use two long branches to make the axels for the wheels, attaching two wheels to each axel. Make sure the wheels will rest outside the wagon frame.

Glue the axles with the wheels onto the bottom of the wagon, using the glue liberally and covering it well with moss.

7   The last step is to fill your wagon with whatever materials or objects you would like. You could make little garden tools or little buckets, brooms, birdcages, and beehives. Decorate the outside of the wagon with pods, moss, leaves, berries, or any natural treasures that appeal to you!

The Gardener's Wagon is another wonderful piece that would be so charming in a whimsical storybook play in a woodland setting. Used along with some of the other pieces shared in our book, the creative and imaginative artist could create a truly enchanted world with endless adventure and surprise!

Imagine the most rustic, earthy
little elf whose gardens are the
envy of all the elfin world.

The Gardener's Potting Shed
with Accessories

The Gardener's Potting Shed is a wonderful piece, so imaginative and charming. Make your potting shed from your vision of the most enchanting garden of all, and it will be beautiful!

YOU'LL NEED:

A   Wood or cardboard for the base

B   Wood, bark, or cardboard for the walls and roof

C   Wood, bark, or twigs for workbenches and chairs

D   Mica for windows

E   Clay for garden pots

Paint for garden pots (optional; not pictured)

Herbs, flowers, and wild grass to hang up to dry (not pictured)

F   Moss, bark, flowers, and leaves for decoration

G   Miniature seed packets made from reduced photos of seed packages

1 If you would like, you can draw out the design of your potting shed first to figure out how you want it to look, or you can make cardboard templates before you begin.

Cut out the base of your shed; it can be square or rectangular. Then cut wall pieces from cardboard, wood, or bark that match the width of the base piece. You can make the wall pieces all the same height or give one wall an interesting angle as shown. In this step, cut only the solid walls; you will make a wall with a window in the next steps. Consider leaving one side open to be able to access the inside of the potting shed.

Lay out your frame. Glue together any walls that won't have any windows , then glue the walls to the base..

2 To make a wall with a window, start with two separate strips of bark or cardboard that are the width of the base piece. Make sure the strips (when glued together) match the height of wall they will adjoin. Cut the shape for the window from the inside of the strips as shown, then glue the strips together to form one solid wall piece.

Glue the window wall in place on the shed frame.

3 Cut a piece of mica a little larger than the window space that will overlap the edge. Then secure the mica piece to the wall, gluing the mica under its overlapping edges so that the glue will not show.

4 Cut out and glue on long strips of wood, bark, or cardboard for trim over the mica window edges, and cover the glue with moss.

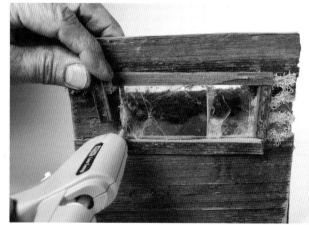

5 Make a workbench or tall table following steps 1–4 for A Fairy Table on page 44; then glue the table to the inside or outside wall of the shed. Since your workbench or table will be supported by a wall on the back, you only need to make one or two legs to provide front support.

Add bracing between the legs of the workbenches and tables, but leave the front areas open.

Glue the workbench to the inside or outside wall of the shed. You can have workbenches or tables along all three walls, along just one wall, or both inside and outside the shed.

6 Make several chairs or stools that your little garden gnome or elf can sit on while he plants new herbs or flowers in his pots and containers. Following steps 1–7 for A Little Chair on pages 37–38, you can make a small chair out of old wire or metal, like a Victorian garden chair, or out of bark and twigs to match your workbench .

7 Over the workbenches and tables, you can also add shelves to store tools, plants, and seed packets. Make the shelves out of wood, twigs, bark, or thick leaves; brace them with twigs or tendrils.

Make tiny pots and garden planters out of clay. When they are dry, paint them or leave them their natural color.

8 Decorate the inside of the little potting shed. Tie small bunches of herbs and wild grass together to hang on the walls; make a wooden or bark barrel or weave a small basket to store tall flowers; add a little chair into another corner and make a rake to rest against a wall; put tiny seeds in open pods and set them on worktables or shelves.

Accessories

POTS AND GARDEN PLANTERS

Make little pots and garden planters from tiny pods or shells; use thin, long strips of bark and leaves to make seedling flats. Make shovels and other tools out of tiny twigs, vines, tendrils, and bark. Weave small baskets from strawberry, wisteria, or other thin vines, and add grapevine handles.

TINY SEED PACKETS

Stock the potting shed with tiny seed packets. To make these, just find a garden seed catalog and photocopy the pictures of the seed packages, reducing the photos down to whatever size you need. Display them on the shelves you've made or set them in vine baskets.

A gazebo is a beautiful
refuge—a place for
dreaming and calming
your spirit.

The Fairyland Gazebo

A gazebo seems like a perfect piece to make if you are going to have a wondrous fairyland world. Your piece can reflect that wonderful place you like to go to in your thoughts when you imagine a lovely garden in a faraway land.

YOU'LL NEED:

A Cardboard or plywood to make the base

B Moss to cover the base

C Vines or coated wire branches for open-air walls

D Tendrils, dried flowers, and grass for decoration

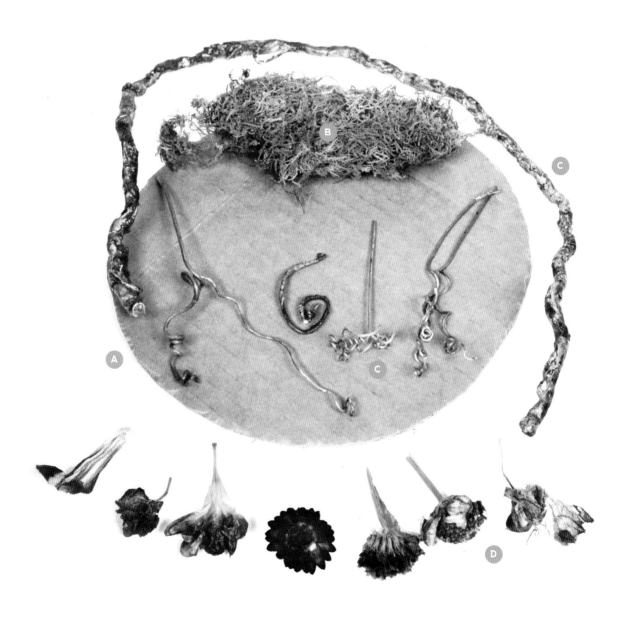

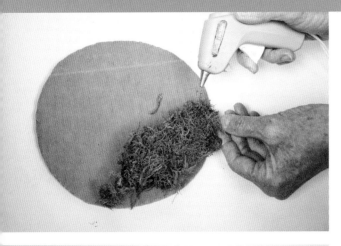

1

For the steps here, we have made a gazebo that is about 12 inches high and 9 inches wide.

Cut a thick piece of cardboard or a piece of thin plywood into a round or oval shape.

Glue thick moss onto the top surface of the base.

2

For the open-air walls of our gazebo, we used coated wire branches. The thinner, curly, tendril-like ends of these branches can be used for embellishments on the outside of the gazebo. However, if this kind of material is not available to you, any kind of vine or branch will do.

Glue the thicker part of the vines around the perimeter of the moss base. Space each branch or vine apart to give the walls an open, summery look, leaving the front part open. After gluing, cover with moss to make your walls sturdier.

3

Join the vines together here and there to create a curvy, intertwined look. Cover each area that you join together with moss.

Continue adding more vines, joining them together in a somewhat random, creative pattern, finally bringing them together at the top of the gazebo.

Check all the areas that you have glued together to make sure they are sturdy, well glued, and covered with moss.

4 Using the coated wire, any kind of bendable wire, or a flexible green vine, form curvy coils to attach here and there along the gazebo walls. Add grapevine or other kinds of tendrils within the walls in different areas to give your gazebo a wispy, magical look. Again, cover the glue with moss.

5 Decorate the gazebo with statice and larkspur flowers, little dried rose buds, and small dried carnations here and there where the vines are joined together. Add a larger, brighter flower at the very top of the gazebo.

6 It would be lovely for a wee little elf and his fairy princess to sit out in your Fairyland Gazebo on the chairs and benches that you've already created.

You could also make a tiny little lantern to hang up at the top of the gazebo. Add small shelves here and there to put candles on for a magical evening. Make a birdcage or harp; add an easel, paints, and brushes. Give your gazebo a storybook look, and it will truly have an enchanted fairytale appeal.

The gentle voice and spirit
in each of our hearts
gives us lovely, peaceful
thoughts to live by.

The Fairyboat Bed

T his piece is one of the most enchanting and beautiful pieces we created for our book—it is one of our favorites. The Fairyboat Bed has wonderful lines and movement. It's a dreamy boat bed—perfect for a prince and his princess!

YOU'LL NEED:

A Cardboard for templates

Bark to cover cardboard frame (not pictured)

B Cattail down for bedding

C Moss for pillows and cushions

D Thin branches, wire vines, or tendrils for the canopy

E Flowers, pods, grapevine tendrils, and shiny silver jewels for decoration

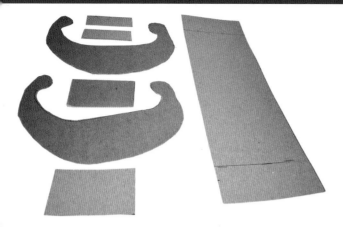

1 Draw the shape you want for your Fairyboat Bed onto cardboard (cereal boxes work well for this). This should include seven pieces: two identical side pieces with curves along both edges, a long rectangular piece for the bottom, and four short rectangular pieces for the headboard and footboard seating. The side piece shapes should be uneven, with one side higher than the other to form a bow.

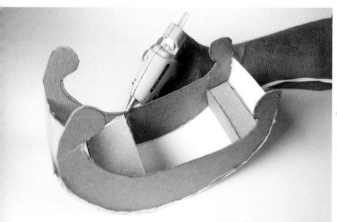

2 Cut the pieces of cardboard out from the designs you've drawn.

Glue the side cardboard pieces to the bottom piece, and cover all visible glue with moss. Try to keep all the edges you are gluing lined up well so that the boat sits evenly and straight.

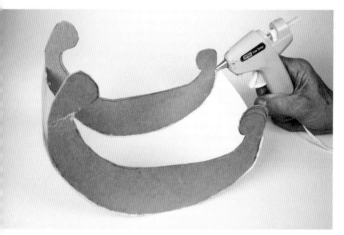

3 Glue in the cardboard pieces for the benches, attaching two seat pieces together at a right angle and then gluing the free edges to the head of the boat bed, resting between the two side pieces. Repeat this step at the opposite, higher side for the bow of the boat.

4 Cover the cardboard with bark, gluing it onto the inside and outside of the Fairyboat Bed and leaving the area for the seat cushions to be embellished with moss.

5 Fill in the bedding for the Fairyboat Bed. We have used soft and beautiful cattail down. Pull small clumps of the down from the stalk and glue them into the open frame in the middle of the bed. The area closest to the headboard should be thicker to resemble pillows.

Glue moss or another soft material onto the front and back of the seats in the Fairyboat Bed.

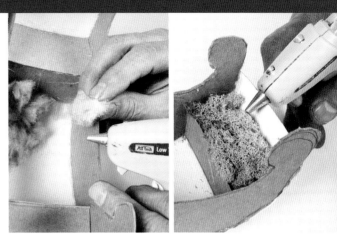

6 Create a beautiful and delicate canopy from thin branches, tendrils, or wire vines. Attach the thicker branches to the four corners of the main part of the bed. Use glue liberally so that these support branches will be sturdy. Then cover the glue with moss.

7 Add more delicate stems with flowers or thin twigs alongside the branches on each corner of the bedding. From there, add the wire vine in a circular design to give the top part of the canopy more movement. Not a lot of glue is needed for these more delicate materials, but it is still important to make sure each area is glued and covered with moss well enough that it holds.

8 Add pretty hydrangea or chamomile flowers here and there to the canopy. To make the bark look more delicate, use lavender buds and bachelor's button petals along the sides of the boat and touches of purple statice, tiny red sumac berries, grapevine tendrils, and interesting pods. Embellish the floating bed with shiny, glittery clusters and crystal-like jewels to make it even more magical. Make little oars by gluing rounded bark onto twigs.

The little people need to go from one enchanted place to another, so what better way to journey to the next hobbit village than in a rustic, rumbly car made of bark and moss!

The Woodland Race Car

Y ou might think that elves or gnomes would never be seen driving a car in their fairy woodland kingdom, but one never knows what the little people of the forest might invent. After all, it is an imaginary, wondrous world where anything can happen, so perhaps little cars do exist for the characters of the woods to travel in!

YOU'LL NEED:

A   Large, curled piece of bark for the car body

B   Various pieces of bark for the frame, wheels, and steering wheel

C   Tendril for gear shift

D   Kelp for the hand brake

E   Thin branch for the steering column

F   Two branches for wheel axles

G   Moss and pods for decoration

1 Find a large, curled piece of bark. You may not find the exact piece as the one we have used for our little car, but something similar will do. You should be able to find a circular piece of bark around fallen branches. Remove it carefully to keep the piece intact.

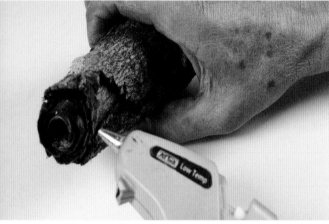

2 To enclose the front of the car, glue a small, circular piece of bark into the nose, using moss to cover any visible glue.

3 You can add long, narrow strips of thin bark over any areas where the pieces don't come together close enough, adding moss to help them stay together.

4 Find an interesting, rustic piece of bark for the back or trunk of the car. It needs to be wide enough to match up to the front shape of the car and long enough to accommodate the back wheels and axle when they are added.

5 Glue a long piece of bark onto the bottom of the car to enclose the rest of the framework. If you don't have one solid piece, use several pieces. Cover any visible glue with moss to strengthen the floor of the car.

6 Add a small, somewhat curled piece of bark for the back of the driver's seat, gluing it inside the car onto the floor.

7 Use a little tendril for a gearshift on one side and a piece of kelp for a hand brake on the other. Add tiny, round pieces of white birch bark on the dashboard for dials.

8 Make a steering wheel for the car by cutting out a circle from a thin bark like eucalyptus, manzanita, or birch. You can also make a cardboard template first, if you'd like, then cover it with bark and moss.

9 Attach a long branch to the right side of the steering wheel, and cover the glue well with moss. Then glue the entire steering wheel column into the car on the floor across from the seat.

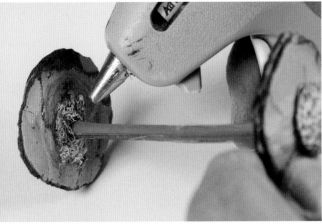

10 Find another sturdy piece of bark to make into circles for the wheels. Cut four identical circular shapes for the wheels and set them aside. Trim two fairly thick branches for the axles; one should be shorter than the other to use in the front of the car where the car body is narrower. Glue the wheels to the ends of the axles, making them sturdier by covering the glue with moss or lichen. Add little acorn caps or hollow pods to the center of the wheels for the hubcaps.

11 Attach each axle, with its wheels, onto the bottom of the car, glueing the longer branch underneath the trunk and the narrower one near the front of the car. Use lots of glue to make sure the axles stay on well enough to support the wheels.

Now you've completed your amazing Woodland Race Car. Your little car will surely make you smile every time you see it, and you will imagine yourself racing through the woods in your little rustic, rumbling automobile!

Where songs are sung more delightfully, lines in a play are spoken with even more wondrous tones, and stories float through the air with melody and drama.

Theater in the Woods

The Theater in the Woods is so enchanting that one might think they have traveled to another land. What a perfect piece to end our book with, one that encourages dreams and the joy of the imagination!

YOU'LL NEED:

A Thick cardboard for frame of theater, trees, and small buildings

B Two lids from cardboard boxes

C Small pieces of corrugated cardboard for roof pieces

D Utility knife

E Thick bark and curled cherry bark pieces

F Acrylic paint

G Paintbrushes

H Pods for footlights

I Flowers, leaves, shells, and pods for decoration

J Moss for theater floor and for covering glue

K Scrapbook paper or photocopied pictures for backdrops

1

Like the boat and several other pieces we've shared with you, cardboard is used for the basic frame of the theater. Find a thick cardboard box. The box we used was 11 inches high, 12 inches wide, and 5 inches deep.

Cut off the bottom and the side that will be the front opening of the stage.

Cut a slot at the back edge of the top piece, about 1/2 inch wide and 10 inches long. This can be used to slide paper or thin cardboard scenery down onto the back of the stage for different stories or plays.

2

Glue the two box lids together, then attach this "foundation" to the sides and back of the frame; the front lid will extend out past the edge of the theater sides. Use the glue liberally to make the connection of the pieces strong. To make the floor even sturdier, you can add 1/2 inch–wide strips of cardboard under the floor pieces all the way around and glue one long piece of cardboard under the floor in the middle of the two lids. Strengthen all of the glued areas with moss.

3

Cut out two smaller cardboard rectangles the same height as the walls and about 3 inches wide. These pieces will make the façade at the front of the theater. Glue the panels to the front sides of the frame and to the floor, extending each panel out halfway past the side. Reinforce the glue with moss.

4   Cut a triangular piece of thick cardboard, 12 inches wide and 5 inches tall at its highest point. The bottom part of the triangle can be slightly rounded with the corners squared to give this piece a more distinct design. Glue this triangle onto the top part of the frame, overlapping the side panels a little. Use the glue liberally so the pieces are attached well, and reinforce with moss.

5   Add a thick layer of moss over the floor of the stage, gluing one section on at a time and covering any visible glue. Be sure to bring the moss all the way out to the edge of the floor to cover the cardboard completely. You can also use pussy willows, leaves, pressed flowers, or bark, or create a mosaic floor out of shells or tiny stones.

6   Cover the façade pieces with thick, textured bark. Add curled bark, unusual pods, small stones, and leaves for embellishments. You can also make a little bark awning to attach to the triangular piece of the façade.

7   Paint a pastoral scene or other scenery on the inside of the back wall or glue on a photo or drawing that you like for the main scenery of the theater.

8   To add a second dimension to the theater, you can make little painted cardboard trees or use real branches with leaves to set on either side of the stage. They should be glued down several inches in front of the back wall of scenery to create a more layered look, just like a real stage.

9   To add yet another layer to the front of the stage, add small, narrow buildings or watchtowers with windows. They can be cut out from thinner cardboard and painted whatever color you would like. You can even make little people standing in the windows. When these are finished, glue them to the floor and to each side panel, and cover the glue with moss. Add open pods to make little footlights on the floor of the stage to bring your theater to life. Attach them along the front of the stage, angled up toward the inner part of the stage. If you are even more enthusiastic, you can attach a string of tiny lights along the front of the stage and put the bulbs into the pods, covering the cord under the moss. When the cord is plugged in, you will have delicate little lights adorning your stage, as magical as fireflies in the summer.

10   Paint the rest of the cardboard with a forest green acrylic paint.

11 Create murals or scenes on the outer side and back walls. You can also decorate the theater with lovely flowers, leaves, pods, moss, and other fanciful embellishments.

This is your first masterpiece and will surely not be your last, because now you are a true fairytale artist! You have created amazing works of art from nature. Perhaps you have found a new and wonderful talent that you want to keep nurturing and developing. The most important thing of all is to believe in yourself and enjoy what you do. Finding the talent and creativity within you is a wondrous and marvelous journey. Thank you for traveling through this artistic adventure with us. We hope you have fun as you continue to discover the magic of Fairyland!

Tower Observatory

The Fairy Castle

Mailbox

Kitchen Stove

Roof Tiles

Art Studio

Checkerboard

Kitchen Herbs

Bathroom Mirror

Fairy Bed

The Fairy House

Stone Tower

Little Chair

Bathroom Sink

Cello with Chair

Dining Room

Staircase

Kitchen

Appendix A: Natural Materials

Here is an extensive list of natural materials that you can use in your art.

Flowers

Allium

Azalea

Bachelor's button

Black-eyed Susan

Bleeding heart

Calendula

California poppy

Calla lily

Campanula

Canterbury bell

Carnation

Chrysanthemum

Columbine

Coreopsis

Cosmos

Crocus

Daffodil

Dahlia

Daisy

Delphinium

Forget-me-not

Fuchsia

Gladiola

Grape

Hibiscus

Hollyhock

Hop plant

Hyacinth

Hydrangea

Iceland poppy

Iris

Lantana

Lilac

Marigold

Morning glory

Narcissus

Nasturtium

Pansy

Peony

Periwinkle

Primrose

Purple coneflower

Rhododendron

Rose

Stock

Sunflower

Sweet pea

Sweet William

Tea roses

Tulips

Wild roses

Zinnia

Pods

Acacia

Acorn

Agave

Annatto

Australian gum tree

Cottonwood

Crepe myrtle

Curly and flat protea

Dried senna

Dried thistle

Eucalyptus

Flax

Hakea

Jacaranda

Lotus

Magnolia

Mahogany

Milkweed

Palm Tree

Poppy

Putka

Herbs

Angelica

Anise

Basil

Bergamot

Borage

Calendula

Catnip

Chamomile

Chervil

Comfrey

Coriander

English thyme

Fennel

French tarragon

Hyssop

Lady's mantle

Lamb's ear leaves

Lavender

Lemon grass

Lemon verbena

Marshmallow

Meadowsweet

Mint

Mullein leaves

Oregano

Rosemary

Rue

Sage

Sorrel

Sweet cicely

Tansy

Valerian

Wild geranium

Wild ginger

Yarrow

Leaves

Bay

Fig

Gingko

Maple

Mint

Mulberry

Sassafras

Branches

Alder

Birch

Chestnut

Dogwood

Eucalyptus

Fig

Grapevine

Jacaranda

Manzanita

Crepe Myrtle

Oak

Poplar

Willow

Winged elm

Wisteria

Miscellaneous

Here is a list of other kinds of materials that can be used in nature art. This is somewhat of a miscellaneous category, but all of these options will add curious, wondrous detail to your natural pieces.

Bark

Cinnamon sticks

Clover

Dried oranges, lemons, and limes

Dried mushrooms

Dried quince slices

Egyptian reed

Feathers

Holly, pepper, and salal berries

Kelp

Lichen

Mica

Moss: natural green, pink, brown, Chartreuse, Old man's beard

Onion and eggplant skins

Pussy willow

Rose hips

Seaweed

Shells

Starfish

Stones

Seeds

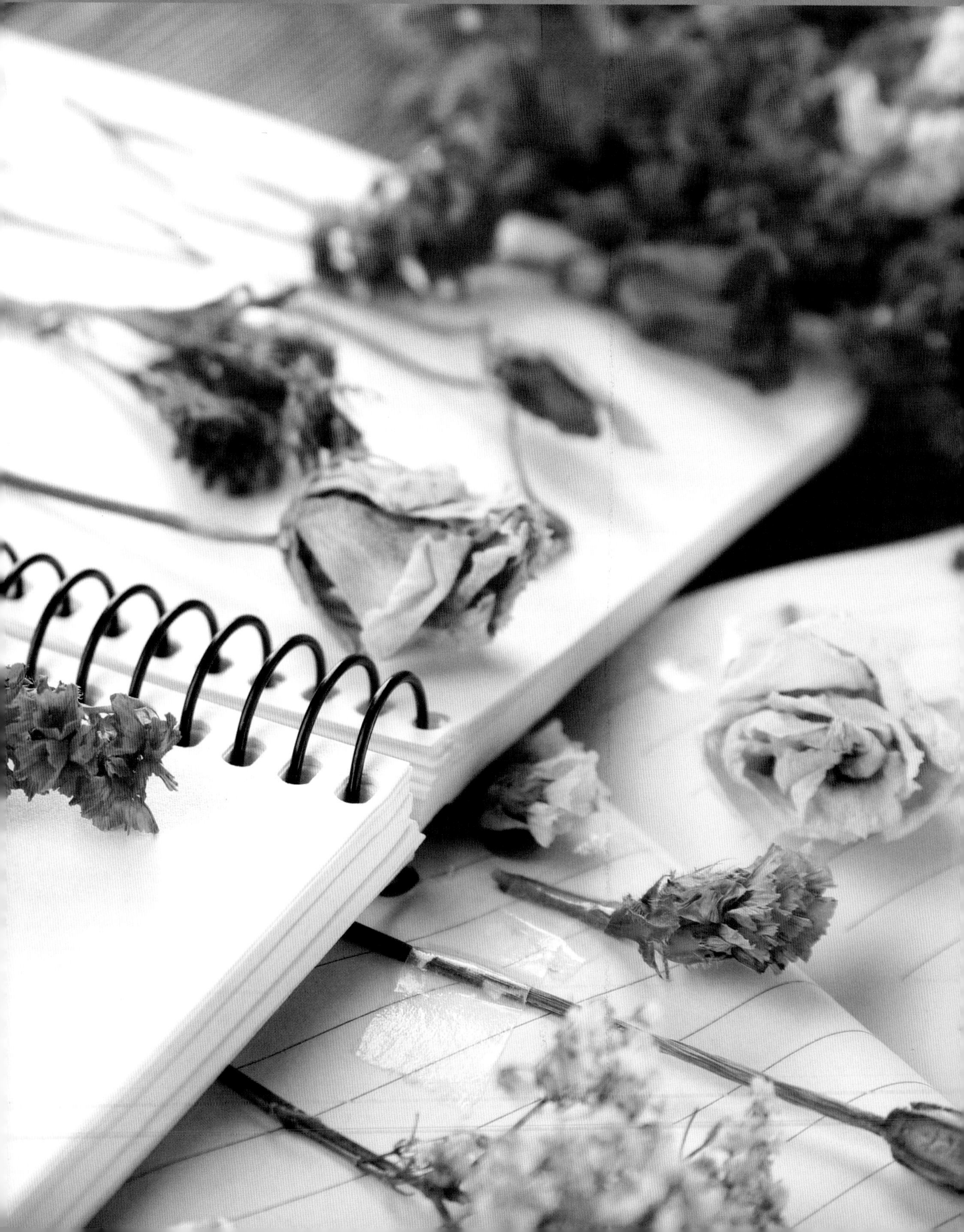

Appendix B: Resources

In this section, we will share with you information about various companies and suppliers who have natural materials that you can order online or purchase in-store if you live near their place of business. We suggest researching a little on your own, too, to find other resources for these materials.

Some companies just offer one kind of product, such as dried or pressed flowers or an unusual variety of shells; others offer a larger range of natural products.

To find the different tools you will need to make nature art, most craft or hardware stores will carry those supplies. Glue guns, glue sticks, scissors, pruners, and tweezers can all be purchased at these stores as well as at department stores like Fred Meyer and Lowe's.

Here we list some of the companies we use, their websites, and the types of products they sell:

COLUMBIA PINECONES & BOTANICALS
- www.pinecones.com
- Pinecones, pods, branches, lichen, pebbles, and shells

PINECONES & PODZ
- www.pineconesandpodz.com
- Pinecones and pods

DRIED FLOWERS DIRECT
- www.driedflowersdirect.com
- Dried flowers

SOURCING NORTHWEST
- www.sourcingnorthwest.com
- Foliage, moss, lichen, dried flowers, herbs, and pinecones

KNUD NIELSEN COMPANY, INC.
- www.knudnielsen.com
- Flowers, berries, branches, bamboo, feathers, foliage, pinecones, moss, leaves, and pods

DRIED FLOWERS "R" US
- www.driedflowersrus.com
- Bamboo, branches, flowers, ferns, grass, moss, pinecones, and foliage

HAMMELMANS DRIED FLORAL
- www.hammelmans.com
- Dried and fresh flowers

MICHAELS CRAFT STORE
- www.michaels.com
- Dried and pressed flowers, branches, moss, lichen, leaf skeletons, shells, sea glass, stones, and pods

NATURE'S PRESSED FLOWERS
- www.naturespressed.com
- Flowers, foliage, ferns, grass, herbs, flower stalks, and flower presses

NETTLETON HOLLOW
- www.nettletonhollow.com
- Branches, foliage, flowers, dried fruits, pods, and grass

OZARK QUALITY PRODUCTS
- www.ozarkquality.com
- Pods, pinecones, grass, moss, and vines

DRIED NATURALS
- www.driednaturals.com
- Flowers, greenery, vines, moss, lichen, branches, and straw products

COMPANIES ON ETSY (WWW.ETSY.COM)

PEBBY'S JOY
- www.etsy.com/shop/PebbysJoy
- Shells

NORTH SEA TREASURES
- www.etsy.com/shop/NorthSeaTreasures
- Sea glass, sea china pieces, stones, and shells

KIMONOS FEATHERS
- www.etsy.com/shop/KimonosFeathers
- Feathers and floral decorative items

LAUGHING COYOTE FIBER
- www.etsy.com/shop/LaughingCoyoteFiber
- Natural and hand-dyed alpaca fiber and fleece

BETULLA
- www.etsy.com/shop/Betulla
- Antique buttons, ribbons, and millinery supplies

ABOUT THE ARTISTS

Mike and Debbie Schramer are largely self-taught artists but grew up in very creative and fascinating families of musicians, composers, artists, writers, inventors, and other amazing people. Their collaborative artwork began within the first few months of their marriage when they gathered natural materials and brought them into their home, creating small, curious habitats. It seemed like an unusual occupation for two newlyweds, but it was magical and intriguing. Their artistic abilities emerged again later while raising their two sons. This talented, visionary artist couple has truly had an amazing array of experiences in their art career, giving them a unique ability and sensitivity to teach and share their knowledge and love of art with others.

As Mike and Debbie's art developed, their fairy furniture was featured in many books, magazines, newspapers, shops, and galleries. After a feature story in *Victoria* magazine in 1991, the excitement surrounding their art really took off. So Debbie and Mike created Whimsical Twigs, their own art company, to make their business official. Their pieces were shown at major gift shows, art festivals, art auctions, and museums; many collectors started buying their art. In 1995, the Schramers were invited by Rebecca Hoffberger, director of the American Visionary Art Museum (AVAM), to show their nature art in their first year-long exhibit, "The Tree of Life." Their Fairy Treehouse was voted the fourth favorite work of art out of the four hundred works in the museum's inaugural exhibit. In 2012, the Schramers' nature art was featured in a special display at AVAM in a second year-long exhibit, entitled "The Art of Storytelling." AVAM is now one of the top ten museums in the United States.

The Schramers currently live in Salt Lake City, Utah, where they create their art and also collect vintage and antique objects to use in their pieces. Their travels take them to exhibit their creations and collections at art, vintage, and antique shows. As artists and teachers, the Schramers have always believed in encouraging the natural creativity of others, so they are very excited to share their years of experience in teaching art in *Fairy House*. Mike and Debbie are always creating new and amazing works of art and experimenting with different mediums and materials. However, their first inspiration for their art will always be the beauty of nature, no matter the medium. For more fun and information on the artists and their work, visit:

www.fairyhousethebook.etsy.com
www.fairyhousethebook.blogspot.com
www.pinterest.com/fairyhousebook
www.facebook.com/fairyhousethebook
www.enchantedtreehousemovie.com

ABOUT FAMILIUS

Welcome to a place where mothers and fathers are celebrated, not belittled. Where values are at the core of happy family life. Where boo-boos are still kissed, cake beaters are still licked, and mistakes are still okay. Welcome to a place where books—and family—are beautiful. Familius: a book publisher dedicated to helping families be happy.

VISIT OUR WEBSITE: WWW.FAMILIUS.COM

Our website is a different kind of place. Get inspired, read articles, discover books, watch videos, connect with our family experts, download books and apps and audiobooks, and along the way, discover how values and happy family life go together.

JOIN OUR FAMILY

There are lots of ways to connect with us! Subscribe to our newsletters at www.familius.com to receive uplifting daily inspiration, essays from our Pater Familius, a free ebook every month, and the first word on special discounts and Familius news.

BECOME AN EXPERT

Familius authors and other established writers interested in helping families be happy are invited to join our family and contribute online content. If you have something important to say on the family, join our expert community by applying at:

www.familius.com/apply-to-become-a-familius-expert

GET BULK DISCOUNTS

If you feel a few friends and family might benefit from what you've read, let us know and we'll be happy to provide you with quantity discounts. Simply email us at specialorders@familius.com.

Website: www.familius.com
Facebook: www.facebook.com/paterfamilius
Twitter: @familiustalk, @paterfamilius1
Pinterest: www.pinterest.com/familius

FAMILIUS

The most important work you ever do will be within the walls of your own home.